HAUNTED
HUDDERSFIELD

HAUNTED
HUDDERSFIELD

Kai Roberts

The History Press

First published 2012

The History Press
The Mill, Brimscombe Port
Stroud, Gloucestershire, GL5 2QG
www.thehistorypress.co.uk

ISBN 978 0 7524 6790 0
Typesetting and origination by The History Press
Manufacturing managed by Jellyfish Print Solutions Ltd
Printed in India.

Contents

Acknowledgements & Introduction

THE author would like to thank the staff of Huddersfield Local Studies Library, as well as Andy Roberts, Helen Roberts, Phil Roper, Caitlin Sagan and Stephen Wade.

SITUATED at the confluence of the Holme and Colne Valleys, Huddersfield is one of the South Pennines' largest towns. Like so many settlements in this area, it really began to grow during the Industrial Revolution but whilst many former mill towns have since sidled into stagnation, Huddersfield is still generally acknowledged as one of the most handsome and vibrant destinations in the region. The town itself features countless fine examples of Victorian municipal architecture, whilst the surrounding topography – dominated by the landmark of Castle Hill – is an archetypal Pennine landscape.

To the south and west of the town, the further reaches of the Holme and Colne Valley rise into vast tracts of brooding, grit-stone moorland, forming the northern fringes of the Dark Park. Although this terrain is often forbidding, it possesses an austere beauty and visitors have long been captivated by these wild uplands. The Holme Valley is especially associated with tourism, as for thirty-seven years it was the setting for the popular BBC sitcom *Last of the Summer Wine*, and the area around Holmfirth is frequently referred to as 'Summer Wine Country'.

The valleys themselves are dominated by a curious patchwork of ancient seventeenth-century timber-framed halls, eighteenth-century weavers' cottages, nineteenth-century terraces and modern housing – often all clinging like limpets to the steep flanks. Relics of the Industrial Revolution abound, from renovated mills to derelict factories, whilst both railways and canals snake along the valley floors. Many hillsides are scarred by ancient quarrying and the eastern edge of the area was once home to thriving mining enterprises, the decline of which is still a recent and painful memory.

It is an evocative landscape, in which both untamed countryside and human history press close against modernity. This is precisely the sort of environment in which rumours of the supernatural thrive. Yet unlike neighbouring areas such as Saddleworth and Calderdale, the Huddersfield region has been comparatively overlooked in surveys of the paranormal. The only book to have ever devoted its attention to such matters was Philip Ahier's well-respected *Legends and Traditions of Huddersfield and Its District*, published in 1943. Sadly, this tome is long since out of print and unavailable to many.

Of course, in this supposedly rational and enlightened age, some people might question why the lack of such a compendium matters. After all, science has long since banished the supernatural to the realms of fiction and fancy. What value is there in compiling reports of ghostly experiences when, to many, these accounts have little factual merit? Yet much as it is not obligatory to believe in God to study theology, it is not necessary to believe in the supernatural to consider it a topic worthy of discussion, which can reveal a great deal about the human condition and man's relationship with his environment and past.

The truth is, humans have always had anomalous experiences which they interpret in supernatural terms, and continue to do so even though the religious framework which supported such explanations is no longer a dominant force in many people's lives. Unless we wish to dismiss the testimony of countless individuals as falsehood, we have to accept that these anomalous experiences do occur and that they are phenomenologically valid. Whilst the experience may not be causally produced by any supernatural agency, the fact that they are consistently understood by the subjects in those terms indicates something significant.

Many sceptics have sneered that a belief in the supernatural represents a longing for a comforting belief in the afterlife. However, whilst this might be a motivation in some cases, it is largely a glib and patronising analysis that says more about the existential concerns of the accuser than the accused. Rather, it seems that ghosts evolve as a response to environmental factors, both conscious and unconscious. They are personifications of the spirit of place, embodying a need to see the past as immanent in the present and our environment as a living, vital presence in our lives.

Such sensibilities are being increasingly eroded by the ceaseless march of modernity and for many, a belief in the supernatural is one response to a process which severs man from his natural habitat and modes of thought. As such, ghost stories tell us how people feel about a place, how they respond to the myriad subtle inputs which create the ineffable atmosphere of any given location; and even if we do not accept the existence of the supernatural, we can recognise a ghost as a valuable anthropomorphic symbol of its supposed haunt.

A great deal can be inferred about our psychological preoccupations from the motifs that people continue to attach to the supernatural. Some have suggested that the frequency of these images supports there being some objective truth to the supernatural experiences in question. However, a more circumspect explanation is that the recurrence of certain iconography in the stories collected here suggests that these archetypes persist in the collective unconscious as culturally appropriate symbols associated with fringe experiences.

Of course, tragic death is the trope most commonly connected with hauntings but the precise mode of such death is instructive. In an area where industry was such a dominant force in people's lives, it is scarcely surprising to find that industrial accidents loom large in many of these narratives. Equally, bitterly fought conflicts such as the English Civil Wars and the Luddite uprising have clearly left a psychic mark on the region. We also find numerous instances of nationally common motifs, such as White Ladies, spectral horsemen, ghost flyers and headless or faceless apparitions.

Ultimately, it seems that no matter how much paranormal speculation may be discredited in the eyes of modern science, people will continue to have experiences which they feel can only be described as supernatural. As humans, we cannot escape our own history and environment, nor can we healthily suppress the need to personify it in accordance to enduring archetypes. To quote Julian Wolfrey, 'All forms of narrative are spectral to some extent ... to tell a story is always to invoke ghosts, to open a space through which something other returns.' And as another wise man once said, you do not need to believe in ghosts to be afraid of them.

Kai Roberts, 2012

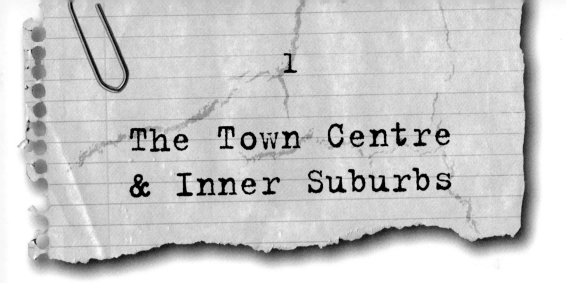

1

The Town Centre & Inner Suburbs

Church of St Thomas, Longroyd Bridge

The Church of St Thomas on Manchester Road is far from an ancient structure. It was erected between 1857 and 1859 according to a design by Sir George Gilbert Scott, one of the most prolific architects of the nineteenth century. In 1929, when the following events occurred, it would've been even younger. Yet evidently the connection between churches and the supernatural in our collective psyche is strong enough for even the most modern examples to seem an appropriate focus for spiritual manifestations.

During the early weeks of September 1929, rumours began to circulate that every evening an apparition of a White Lady 'appeared at the west door of St Thomas's Church'. These reports were so prevalent that increasingly crowds began to gather outside the church, and by the night of 11 September, a horde of almost 2,000 people assembled between nine o'clock and midnight. The throng was so large that it obstructed traffic on Manchester Road and the police were forced to intervene to maintain order.

Contemporary accounts indicate that men, women and children of all ages were present; some curious, some terrified, some sceptical and some bullish. The atmosphere was described as 'strained', but the amassed onlookers were not disappointed and the ghost duly put in an appearance. One journalist reported seeing, 'A figure in white… it swayed backwards and forwards exercising a wonderful fascination over the gaping crowd,' whilst a spectator commented, 'If it wasn't a ghost it was for all the world like one. It looked like the figure of a woman dressed in white. It was really weird.'

The crowd's reaction was mass hysteria. Some even threw stones at the vision, although what they expected such an act to achieve against an incorporeal entity is not clear. The following day, Mr Hampshire, the church sexton, was furious at the damage caused. 'It is a lot of nonsense and I am surprised there should be such a lot of silly people about,' he said. As far as Mr Hampshire was concerned, the 'ghost' was nothing more than an optical illusion created by a gas lamp on Bankfield Road shining through trees onto the western door.

This prosaic explanation notwithstanding, an even larger crowd congregated

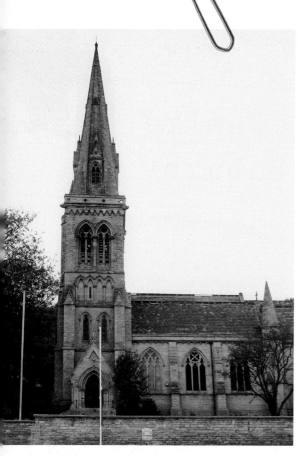

Church of St Thomas, Longroyd Bridge.

the following night. Traffic was again obstructed, whilst one man fainted and a child was knocked down in the chaos. Perhaps shy of this increased attention, the apparition did not satisfy its audience again and soon children were daring each other to approach the church, whilst young men stalked the graveyard in an effort to impress their girlfriends. To persuade the crowd to disperse, the police began showing people up to the door and allowing them to touch it, in order to reassure them that nothing untoward was lurking in the shadows.

The authorities and local press publicly emphasised the 'optical illusion' explanation, and on subsequent nights the crowds dwindled. However, it was not entirely the

end of the matter and 'ghost-hunting' in the vicinity of the church remained a popular local pastime for some while thereafter. The following week a thirty-six-year-old labourer called Edwin Taylor was arrested for disorderly conduct after attacking a man named James Speight in the churchyard, believing him to be the ghost.

Whether it was an authentic apparition or merely a simulacrum, few ghosts in Huddersfield history have caused such a fuss.

The Grand Picture Theatre, Manchester Road

Today, only the façade of this distinguished building remains, but it still presents an imposing sight at the junction of Manchester Road with the town centre ring road. It was originally constructed in 1921 as a cinema and in 1929 became only the second of Huddersfield's many film houses to be wired for sound. However, following the decline in the popularity of such establishments, it was transformed into a bingo hall known as Sheridan Rooms around 1957.

Perhaps the building's most famous and fondly remembered incarnation came in 1972, when it was converted into a venue and nightclub called Ivanhoe's. On Christmas Day 1977, it was the scene of two concerts by legendary punk band, the Sex Pistols, the first of which was a matinee performance played as a benefit gig for the children of striking fire fighters! The evening show, meanwhile, proved to be the band's final British appearance with their original line-up, although nobody knew it at the time.

Not many months after this celebrated event, Ivanhoe's was drawing attention for an altogether different reason. In April 1978, reports began to circulate that the building was haunted by a ghost that only harassed men. One night after closing, two bouncers – scarcely the most suggestible of people – heard footsteps from the balcony and, fearing a customer had been locked in, conducted a thorough search of the venue but failed to find anything.

Some time later, the bouncers heard the footsteps again but still they failed to find their source. When they heard the sound a third time, they began to suspect that somebody was deliberately hiding in the building and called the police. However, despite the use of a sniffer dog, the police search did not locate an intruder either. More curiously still, the normally obedient police dog refused all directions and incentives to enter the balcony area.

Owner Paul Davies and promoter Derek Parkin subsequently heard the balcony footsteps whilst they were working alone in the building one evening. Mr Parkin told the *Huddersfield Daily Examiner:*

We went all over the building but could find nothing. Since then I have avoided the place and only go up there during the day. The previous owner, Ken Sewell, told me he has heard footsteps too. If I

The Grand Theatre.

have to go up there for anything when the place is empty I now take a girl with me because the story is that a female has never heard it.

Days later, the theory that only men could sense the ghost was rebutted by cleaner Madeline Dannatt. She informed the local press that she had heard the phenomenon on many occasions, especially on the balcony, as had a woman who worked in an office on the same floor. Mysterious footsteps were a regular occurrence, but Mrs Dannatt also described seeing doors open and close by themselves, and once hearing the sound of breaking glass without any obvious source.

Rumours amongst employees at Ivanhoe's attributed the disturbances to one of two individuals. The first was a cinema projectionist who had died on the balcony whilst showing a reel; the second was a bingo winner who had passed away before she'd been able to receive her prize money. Staff gossip held that this elderly lady had scored such a large win that the company was unable to pay out for several days, during which period she died and now haunted the former bingo hall, still waiting to collect her due.

Mrs Dannatt also wondered if the ghost might not have become more active in protest at what was being done to that once bustling area of the town, as many surrounding buildings were lost beneath the new ring road layout. She said, 'There used to be a thriving community here and the people were known as Top Enders. But it was all demolished to make way for redevelopment.' Mrs Dannatt even suggested that it may have been the ghost of St Thomas's Church itself, returned to express its displeasure.

The Zetland Hotel, Queensgate

Named in honour of the Earl of Zetland, this handsome edifice was erected on Queensgate in 1847 and subsequently lent its name to an adjoining street, at the junction of which it still stands. Although it has long been known as a haunt of students rather than spirits, the ghostly experiences reported at the hostelry are particularly interesting in that they come from two independent witnesses, almost half a century apart, neither of whom could have known of the other's account. Such material gives credence to the supposition that supernatural encounters are the result of some objective, anomalous phenomenon.

The first public report occurred in 1996, when, for a brief period, the Zetland was masquerading as a faux-Irish bar called O'Neill's. Barman Paul Booth described the sort of run-of-the-mill poltergeist activity common to many pubs, including strange noises after closing, finding all the ashtrays turned upside down overnight, and chairs mysteriously stacked on the stairs. In its own right, this is relatively uninteresting fare; it only acquires significance in view of another report some fourteen years later.

In 2010, a popular nostalgic periodical published the recollections of Mike Silkstone, who had worked behind the bar at the Zetland in the late 1950s. In those days, it was something of a riotous establishment presided over by an alcoholic landlady named Mary but affectionately referred to as 'Mummy'. The writer recalls that she often used to emerge from errands in the cellar sobbing and telling anybody who'd listen that she'd seen 'him' again. After a drink to calm her nerves, she'd explain that 'he' was 'a young solider. He's very unhappy – but he likes to talk to Mummy'. However,

The Zetland Hotel.

Following the closure of the cinema in 1998, the building was the site of a vigil by a team of paranormal investigators who'd received reports of supernatural activity from several people who'd worked there. More than a decade later, Mike Silkstone also mentions that during the 1950s, the ghost of a music hall performer who'd often taken the stage at the Theatre Royal and had died whilst enjoying a pre-show tipple in a pub nearby, had sometimes been seen in the area. The correspondences keep accumulating.

Beast Market

she could never be drawn on the topics of their conversations.

Instructively, the grand building next door to the Zetland had once been home to many a soldier. It was constructed in 1846 as a riding school and for several months of the year styled itself the Theatre Royal, accommodating touring circuses and shows. More relevantly, it was also used as a base for the 2nd West Yorkshire Yeoman Cavalry and subsequently the 6th West Yorkshire Rifle Volunteers, who held their armoury there from 1861 until 1901. Could 'Mummy's' soldier have had his origin in either of these two regiments?

The building went through many further changes after that. In 1902, it was purchased by the Northern Theatre Company and used exclusively as a music hall known as the New Hipperdrome and Opera House. It became the Tudor Cinema in 1930 and the Cannon Cinema thereafter, finally closing its doors in 1998 due to bankruptcy. It has since housed nightclubs such as the Rat & Parrot and Livingstone's, but at the time of writing, this historic structure stands boarded-up and empty.

Huddersfield's weekly market was established in 1671 by royal charter from King Charles II, and over the next couple of decades various 'speciality' markets became associated with different areas of the town. The street known today as Beast Market was the site of the cattle market until 1881, when a new location was found. Doubtless the area has seen many disputes over ownership down the years, but perhaps the most extraordinary came in March 1976, when two neighbouring businesses quarrelled over possession of a ghost.

It began when staff at the Buccaneer Fish Bar and Restaurant (long since closed) reported a number of strange occurrences to the *Huddersfield Daily Examiner*. They described typical poltergeist activity such as displaced objects, slamming doors and flickering lights. Many employees noticed cold spots in the building, whilst on one occasion manageress Sadie Cahill and a waitresses were overcome by a profound sense of despair, which led the latter to sob uncontrollably.

There were also more sinister disturbances. Waitress Betty Liddle received a

Beast Market.

employees had also seen the ghost and they all described a grey-haired old man.

Many people would've been glad to see the back of such a noisy spirit, but not Mrs Broadbent. She was positively dismayed at the prospect of the exorcism at the Buccaneer: 'I have heard that the staff there have got a medium in, but I hope they don't frighten him away. He's a very nice old ghost and has never done us any harm.' Sadly, it is not documented whether the mooted exorcism went ahead, nor whether the spectre continued its residency in Beast Market or returned to the bosom of its former home in Kirkgate.

shock when she was setting the tables and discovered a perfectly normal fork she'd laid out only moments before had been bent violently out of shape. The sound of 'dragging footsteps' was regularly heard from empty rooms and one girl even felt an incorporeal hand placed on her shoulder.

Mrs Calhill was forced to admit, 'The last fortnight has been worse than ever… One night I called the police to search the place but they found nothing. The girls are terrified.' In desperation, owner Barrie Naylor contacted a medium to 'exorcise' the premises. The press recorded that he visited the restaurant and conducted a vigil until three o'clock in the morning, although he did not take any further action on that occasion.

Following the report of the medium's visit, the *Huddersfield Daily Examiner* was contacted by Joan Broadbent, proprietor of Ioan Wholesalers in Kirkgate, which backed on to the Buccaneer. She told them, 'That's our ghost! We have been having incidents like that for years – hearing footsteps and noises when there is no one there, hearing bumps and crashes upstairs at night.' Mrs Broadbent added that several

The Cloth Hall

Apart from the name of Cloth Hall Street, little remains of this building in its original location at the centre of the town, although its former entrance hall now stands in Ravensknowle Park. Constructed in 1766 to accommodate textile merchants seeking to trade their wares on market day, the Cloth Hall was a two-storey circular edifice with a total circumference of half a mile. Curiously, it had been built from red brick rather than the ashlar sandstone typical of the town, and during its lifetime the hall was variously described as the 'Huddersfield Wonder' and 'the ugliest public building in Yorkshire'.

In its heyday, several hundred traders conducted business at the Cloth Hall, although the building was only open on Tuesdays (market day) between eight o'clock in the morning and noon, then again from three until five in the afternoon. A bell was rung to signal closing but nonetheless, over the years at least twenty-one individuals found themselves locked in and the turnkey demanded a substantial gratuity for release.

As the textile industry changed in the second half of the nineteenth century, the Cloth Hall's fortunes declined and although the building was used as a general market in later years, it was ultimately left to stand idle and increasingly derelict. The town council had it demolished in 1930, initially to make way for a new library, but when they realised its market value, they leased the land and the Ritz Cinema was constructed on the site. In 1983, this too was torn down and now retail premises, including Sainsbury's, occupy the area.

Several ghosts were reputed to haunt the Cloth Hall in its prime. The first was a suicide victim, a manufacturer who had hanged himself in the building sometime in the late eighteenth century. Nothing else is recorded about this spectre's origins or even its supposed activities. Indeed, the spirits of suicide victims are a generic motif in English folklore and perhaps this narrative is little more than that. Certainly, the other apparitions' tales seem more extensively developed.

One was known as Old Mike, who had been employed as one of the first turnkeys at the Cloth Hall and continued to revisit his former workplace long after his death. However, Old Mike's spirit seems to have become a considerable source of annoyance to the living tenants of the building and all manner of mischief was attributed to him, especially jumbling up the manufacturers' cloth. Such was their displeasure at this behaviour that in 1793, the vicar of Huddersfield was commissioned to exorcise the building. Curiously, the success of his intervention only seems to have lasted for a period of sixty years.

Former entrance to the Cloth Hall, now re-erected in Ravensknowle Park.

The final phantom to haunt the Cloth Hall belonged to an Irishman named Bernard Flanagan, who in 1789 got lost in the labyrinthine corridors of the building and expired in unrecorded circumstances before he was able to escape. But whilst Flanagan may have been trapped in the Cloth Hall in life, he was rather more peripatetic in death and his ghost was known to roam beyond the hall's confines, surprising the residents of nearby shops and houses with his sudden appearances.

Such was the strength of popular belief in the Cloth Hall's assortment of spirits that on 4 October 1853, when a merchant found himself locked in the building and attempted to summon assistance, pandemonium ensued. The unfortunate gentleman rang the bell on several occasions and gestured from one of the upper windows, but the locals could not think beyond the possibility of a ghost and soon a huge crowd had assembled hoping to catch a glimpse of the manifestation. It was some considerable time before a sceptical member of the assembled throng had the sense to summon the turnkey to investigate further.

The Ghost of New Street

Although the Cloth Hall was razed in 1930, its displaced spectres may well have found new premises to disturb. The ghost of Bernard Flanagan was certainly not tied to the structure and he could be the apparition that has troubled the environs of New Street, adjacent to Cloth Hall Street, over the years. This phantom caused quite a fuss in 1979 when it was reported to the *Huddersfield Daily Examiner* by Ken Thompson and Steve Lloyd, proprietors of a hair salon on the street. Mr Lloyd explained:

New Street, Huddersfield.

When you are alone in the room at night, it feels as if there is a presence with you. All you see is a shape pass behind you in the mirror and when you turn around there is no one there. It has never done any harm – it just makes its presence known.

Following these revelations, other people who worked in shops and offices around New Street came forward to report similar experiences. One added that it had been associated with one of the adjoining yards since the 1930s – a suggestive date perhaps?

The Bedtime Mangle

Supernatural activity of a more unnerving character was recorded at No. 4 Lockwood's Yard, off Upperhead Row. These buildings have since been demolished but stood roughly where the bus station is today. Many years earlier, in 1951, they had belonged to the Huddersfield Corporation and despite their dilapidated state, the organisation was temporarily forced to reuse them to ease a housing crisis following the Second World War.

The first new tenants were a young couple with a baby, and to support his family the husband worked a night shift, leaving his wife and child alone in the house. However, he was soon forced to reconsider his position when he returned home each morning to find his wife increasingly terrified. She reported latched doors opening and closing of their own volition and strange, cacophonous sounds in the early hours of the morning, although all the neighbours were in bed.

After resigning his nocturnal employment, the husband soon heard this racket himself, including the sound of chopping wood and a laundry mangle being used. Identifying their source as the cellar, he duly went to investigate, only to find that the noises mysteriously ceased as soon as he descended. He subsequently discovered that whilst the buildings were being refitted for reuse, the Housing Department had removed a large mangle from the cellar of the house.

The young baby also seemed to become a focus of the spirit's attention. On several occasions, the couple noticed their child responding to an unseen presence, lifting its arms playfully into the air as it did when it wanted picking up. This was followed by a more disturbing incident, in which the parents found the child making a choking noise and flailing at its neck, as if trying to dislodge some constricting force.

The breaking point came when the mother was bathing her child in front of the fire, and after turning briefly away to locate a towel, found the baby on the hearthrug several feet away from the bathtub and perilously close to the flames. The family was forced to vacate the premises and move back in with their parents. Later tenants allegedly also reported eerie phenomena, especially untraceable noises in the dead of night, and the house continued to be troubled until it was finally – perhaps mercifully – condemned.

St George's Square

The focal point of St George's Square is undoubtedly the neo-classical façade of the railway station, resplendent with its portico entrance and eight Corinthian columns. It was constructed between 1846 and 1850 as a joint venture between the Huddersfield and Manchester Railway and Canal

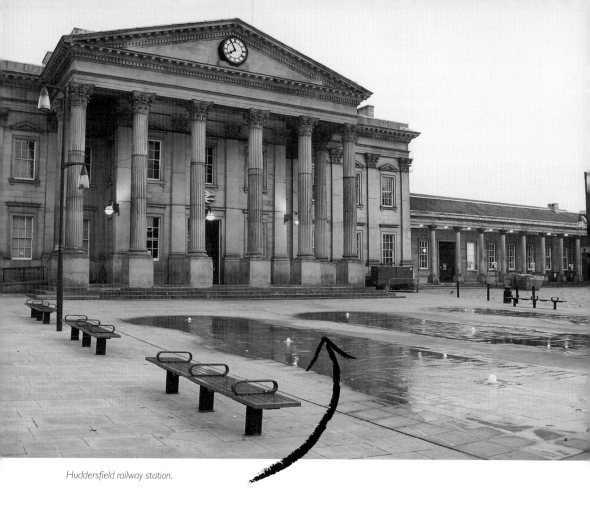

Huddersfield railway station.

Company and the Manchester and Leeds Railway. As such, no expense was spared. The result has been described as 'one of the best early railway stations in England' by the architectural historian Sir Nikolaus Pevsner, and like 'a stately home with trains' by the poet and conservationist, Sir John Betjeman.

In 2008, researcher Stephen Wade collected reports regarding supernatural activity at the station, primarily from the tireless staff who keep the place operational. Various employees have experienced cold spots around the building, whilst a number have heard the sound of threatening laughter on the air and subsequently suffered an accident following the sensation of a nip

or shove from some invisible presence. The time around 11.25 a.m. is rumoured to be particularly unlucky at the station.

Wade notes that workplace folklore ascribes the phenomena to the spirit of a man named Jonah Marr, who had served as a porter at the station in the nineteenth century. Marr was adept at wheedling excessive gratuities out of wealthy passengers and became something of a pariah amongst his peers. Indeed, he was so disliked by his co-workers that when he fell from the platform onto the tracks one day, breaking both his legs, none of them attempted to help him up. His broken limbs never properly set, leaving him crippled and barely able to perform his duties.

Ominously, Marr's ruinous accident is said to have occurred at 11.25 a.m.

Paranormal disturbances have also been reported from other buildings in St George's Square, especially some of the surrounding bars. One licensee told the local press in 1984 that his pumps turned themselves on overnight, leaking valuable beer, whilst strange smells and gusts of air seemed to plague the premises. He claimed to have witnessed objects propelled across the room at his staff by an unseen force, and indicated that one employee had even seen the phantom, which resembled a crooked old man pushing some sort of basket.

The Mechanic's Institution, Northumberland Street

This distinctive building on North-umberland Street was originally constructed in 1861 as the first permanent home for the Huddersfield Mechanic's Institution, a society which later developed into Huddersfield Technical College and ultimately, the University of Huddersfield. The Institution only occupied the Northumberland Street premises until 1883, whereupon the building became the Friendly and Trades Club, in which guise it remained for more than a century. The club was finally dissolved in the early 1990s and after a period of neglect, the property has since been converted into residential apartments.

During its final days, the Friendly and Trades Club was the scene of one of the most credible poltergeist manifestations in the town's history. It began – as so many of these cases seem to – with beer pumps switching themselves on in full view of several members of staff. An electrician was called but he failed to find any fault with the wiring. Curiously, a nine-year-old boy whose parents worked as stewards at the club claimed to have been thinking about the pumps just before the incident.

The disturbances soon began to pile up, their intensity apparently increasing. Caps began to pop off bottles; glasses jumped from the shelves; cutlery danced around the room. One customer was forced to shield himself from an entire salvo of beer bottles which flew over the bar, whilst another was struck by an empty brandy bottle. This phenomena was witnessed by both patrons of the establishment and members of staff, including club official A.D. Dightmas, steward Marian Swales, and handyman Stuart Broadbent.

Huddersfield Daily Examiner journalist Stephen Cliffe was especially convinced by the sincerity of the witnesses. He later wrote, 'I detected only looks of concern – no muffled sniggers or barely concealed smiles,' and described their demeanour as 'pasty and chastened'. Such was the apparent reliability of the accounts, the Society for Psychical Research even expressed an interest: 'This sounds like an authentic case of poltergeist haunting. Things very often fly about and usually the disturbances are associated with a person present.' The last remark is particularly interesting in view of the testimony of the nine-year-old, as children are frequently connected with poltergeist activity.

However, a full investigation into the phenomena was never able to proceed, as all further enquiries into the matter were suppressed. Following Cliffe's report on the haunting in the *Huddersfield Daily Examiner*, his editor was contacted by a municipal councillor who also sat on the committee of the Friendly and Trades Club. Presumably concerned about adverse publicity, he demanded an end to the matter and Mr Cliffe found his planned follow-up vigil at the club abruptly cancelled.

The Old Gas Works

Whilst many are disappearing to gentrification and redevelopment, the decaying industrial hinterlands surrounding any urban centre invariably exude a desolate, forlorn sort of atmosphere. The area around the old Huddersfield gas works, between town and the Galpharm Stadium, is no different. The plant's three gasometers were once an unmistakable feature of the local skyline but two were demolished in 2006, leaving a tract of barren wasteland which, despite numerous schemes and proposals, has yet to be redeveloped.

The ambience is compounded by the murky waters of the Huddersfield Broad Canal, which snakes through the encroaching dereliction en route to join the Calder & Hebble Navigation at Cooper Bridge. Built in 1776, it is the older of the Colne Valley's two canals and like many such waterways, fell into disuse during the early twentieth century. But unlike its younger, narrower brother, it has not enjoyed any significant revival in fortune. The landscape it traverses has little recreational potential and today the canal is primarily associated with untimely death – accidents, suicides, even murder.

The wretched ghost that haunts this territory seems to embody all these associations. Indeed, it may not be the restless spectre of some drowned boatman, but a manifestation of the *genius loci* – the spirit of place incarnate. The tale of this apparition was collected by the writer Stephen Wade, who reports sightings of a limping, crooked figure on the fallow ground of the old gas works. People have also heard a disembodied voice humming some old tune and the distant tap of a walking stick, usually at night as they spill out of the nearby pubs.

Local folklore attributes such phenomena to the ghost of Old Joe, a nineteenth-century canal worker who threw himself into the watery depths when chronic illness left him unable to earn a living. Significantly, some witnesses claim to have seen the indistinct form of a man lurch into the canal yet make no impact on the water. Such an experience conforms to the concept of 'residual haunting', which asserts that ghosts are not the spirits of the dead, but the memory of some traumatic event imprinted on the fabric of a place, mindlessly replayed over and over again to susceptible individuals.

Opposite from top
Mechanics' Institution, Huddersfield.
The Huddersfield Gas Works.

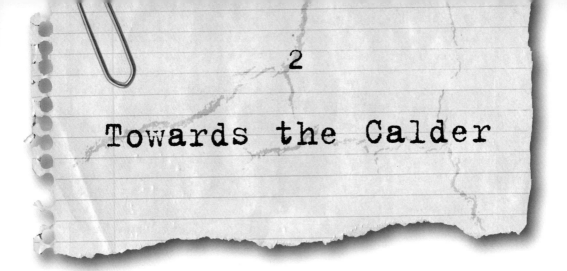

2

Towards the Calder

Sir Richard Beaumont

For centuries, the Beaumont family of Whitley Hall were one of the most venerable dynasties in the Huddersfield region. Indeed, they once practically owned the town, having been granted large tracts of land around the area in the late twelfth century following their contribution to the Third Crusade. But whilst the family continued to enjoy their high status well into the twentieth century, they lost the majority of their holdings in the early 1600s, during the lifetime of one of their most controversial sons, Sir Richard Beaumont, otherwise known as 'Black Dick'.

Whilst his nickname may prompt many a schoolboy snigger today, it was a source of terror to many generations of Kirkheaton children. Nobody knows exactly why Sir Richard was dubbed Black Dick. Local tradition says that it was in memory of his 'black deeds' but as the soubriquet is supposed to have been bequeathed by the King, that seems unlikely. A variety of alternative suggestions have been put forward, including that it referred to his jet-black hair, the colour of his regimental tunic, or even his melancholy disposition.

Certainly on the surface he seems to have led an exemplary life. Born in 1674, he inherited the Beaumont estates aged only five months, which were held in trust by Queen Elizabeth I herself until he reached his majority. He subsequently led a troop of infantry consisting of 200 men for James I, served as a Justice for the Peace and a member of parliament for Pontefract. He was knighted in 1609 and raised to the baronetcy in 1628. Even his tenants seem to have admired him after he founded a free grammar school in Kirkheaton in 1610.

Nonetheless, there remains a murky undercurrent to the life of Sir Richard Beaumont. Much to the exasperation of his peers, he never married or sired legitimate offspring and was well known as a womaniser, with several mistresses recorded. Meanwhile, it is thought the reason he sold off vast swathes of the Beaumont estate was to pay excessive debts incurred through gambling, whilst dark rumours persist that he was involved in highway robbery. In view of such gossip, it is perhaps unsurprising that Black Dick has become one of the most notorious phantoms in the district.

Black Dick's Tower.

Black Dick's Tower

Whitley Hall, the ancestral seat of the Beaumont family, stood on a hillside above the village of Lepton until its destruction in 1951. A dwelling house was first built on the site in the twelfth century, although the last hall was a widely admired Georgian mansion built in the eighteenth century, with gardens designed by Capability Brown. It was finally vacated in 1917, when the Beaumonts decided to relinquish Whitley Park to mineral extraction for the war effort. As a result, the hall became unstable and ultimately had to be demolished.

All that remains of the former estate is an old summerhouse, perched on an elevation, commanding extensive views over the surrounding countryside. Although it was undoubtedly constructed no earlier than the eighteenth century, it has long been known as Black Dick's Tower and local tradition maintains that it was used by Sir Richard as a lookout post for his criminal activities on the nearby roads. A secret underground passage is supposed to have run from the 'tower' to Whitley Hall, by which he could make a quick getaway.

One story claims that following a particularly lucrative raid on a passing stagecoach, a criminal associate attempted to blackmail Sir Richard, threatening to divulge the good baronet's activities to the authorities if he did not hand over some of the loot. The two arranged a rendezvous to discuss terms, to be held in the tunnel between Whitley Hall and the summerhouse on the night of 5 July.

However, the infamous Black Dick had no intention of sharing his spoils and a violent struggle ensued. Alas, despite his skills as a swordsman, in the dark, confined space of the tunnel, Sir Richard quickly lost his advantage and ultimately his life. His skull was struck clean from his body and people say that at midnight on 5 July ever since, the headless ghost of Black Dick can be seen walking the route of the secret tunnel from the summerhouse to Whitley Hall with the severed appendage tucked beneath his arm.

As late as the mid-twentieth century, crowds used to gather in the vicinity of the summerhouse on 5 July, hoping to glimpse Sir Richard's revenant. Yet it seems the story is entirely apocryphal. The 'secret passage' leading from the summerhouse is little more than an old wine cellar compounded by small-scale mining activities following the Beaumonts' departure from Whitley Park. Furthermore, records state that Sir Richard Beaumont died a natural death on 20 October 1631, so where the date of 5 July originates is a mystery.

Some have wondered if Sir Richard's name might have been confused with that of his ancestor Sir Robert Beaumont, who, according to a late-medieval ballad, was beheaded at Crosland Hall in 1341. This act, perpetrated by Sir John de Eland, High Sheriff of Yorkshire, was the opening episode in a revenge saga known as the Elland Feud. Documentary evidence has been discovered to support at least some details of this tradition and whilst the murder of Sir Robert remains unconfirmed, it may well have transpired as the legend claims.

The Ghosts of Whitley Hall

Whitley Hall was supposedly home of the 'bloody hand' of Sir Richard Beaumont, which was kept bricked up behind one of the fireplaces, possibly as a talisman against malign forces. It was not unusual to keep grisly objects of this nature in chimneys. As late as the nineteenth century, such threshold locations were regarded as potential entry points for witches and required 'guardians' to protect them. In this capacity, many unusual items have been discovered concealed in the fabric of old houses; mummified cats, old shoes, nail-clippings or urine of the owner, even human skulls.

But if the item in question did exist, it was clearly ineffectual, for Black Dick was not the only ghost to walk at Whitley Hall. A friend of the Beaumont family witnessed the apparition whilst she was staying at the house some time in the 1880s. Her hosts had departed on an afternoon saunter but owing to the heat of the day, their guest had chosen to remain indoors, writing letters. Glancing up from her correspondence, she was confronted by the sight of a lady in a white dress crossing the room towards a window that opened onto the lawn, at which point the figure vanished.

Local tradition identified this phantom with one of Black Dick's mistresses, perhaps the girl he'd spurned after she'd contracted smallpox and lost her fair complexion. However, it is worth noting that headless ghosts and spectral White Ladies are amongst the oldest, most ubiquitous motifs in English ghost lore. It is possible that such traditions existed in the locality of Whitley Hall long before the lifetime of Sir Richard

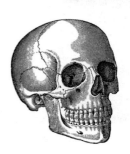

Beaumont and were only associated with his deeds by later generations in search of a narrative. This could certainly explain why the legendary date and method of Black Dick's death differ so markedly from the historical reality.

Church of St John the Baptist, Kirkheaton

The church at Kirkheaton has an ancient provenance. From relics discovered incorporated into the modern structure, historians believe that a chapel was originally founded on the site in the Anglo-Saxon period. When Kirkheaton became a parish in its own right during the thirteenth century, a larger church was constructed. It was substantially renovated in 1828 and again following a fire in 1886. However, parts of the medieval church still remain in the building today.

The most significant remnant from that period is the Beaumont Chapel. Originally constructed as a chantry, it was adopted by the Beaumont family as their private chapel and burial vault following the Reformation. Thankfully, it largely escaped the conflagration of 1886 and one of its centrepieces remains the fine sepulchral monument of Sir Richard Beaumont, a striking effigy of whom lies in repose beneath the painted canopy.

Black Dick's Tomb, Kirkheaton Church.

Local tradition credited this effigy with the power of self-motion and it was believed to sit up whenever the church clock struck midnight. Like so many superstitions associated with Black Dick, this is a trope found frequently in English folklore; similar tales are recorded the length and breadth of the country and the device was memorably employed by Edith Nesbit in her classic ghost story, 'Man-Size In Marble'.

According to Philip Ahier, the belief largely died out following the fire, but the effigy was clearly once held in some awe by the locals. Ahier reports that on one occasion, a man drinking in the nearby Beaumont Arms accepted a challenge to enter the chapel by night and hammer a nail into the image of Sir Richard. However, such was his hurry in the darkness, he unwittingly managed to hammer the nail through his own clothing as well. Upon attempting to leave he found himself sharply dragged back and, thinking Black Dick had risen to claim him, he lost his nerve and bawled in terror until the other members of his party came to his rescue!

Strange noises were also sometimes heard coming from the vault beneath the chapel, where the bones of Sir Richard and many of his ancestors are actually interred.

Local historian Legh Tolson reports that Black Dick's revenant was believed to walk between Whitley Hall and his tomb within the church (in addition to the summerhouse) and the vicinity of St John's was feared by the local children after dark.

Despite his celebrity, Black Dick is one of those legendary ghosts that looms large in the local psyche but is rarely the object of any first-hand witness accounts, especially in the modern period. Perhaps the only suggestion of his presence in recent decades comes from 1975, when builders working late refurbishing a cottage at Gawthorpe Green fled from their job following a confrontation with the unknown. The exact nature of the apparition is not recorded but it is instructive that the hamlet lies directly between Whitley Hall and the church at Kirkheaton – perhaps even on Black Dick's route between the two.

The Royal & Ancient, Colne Bridge

Although countless pubs try to draw in customers with tales of supernatural activity, the Royal & Ancient on Dalton Bank Road at Colne Bridge has better reason than most for its haunted reputation. Although the building itself only dates from the 1930s, it replaced an earlier hostelry known as the Spinners Arms, which, on 14 February 1818, witnessed one of the worst industrial disasters of the age.

At the time, a cotton mill owned by Thomas and Law Atkinson stood opposite the Spinners Arms. As was still customary at this point in history, the mill operated continuously twenty-four hours a day in order to maximise profits. During night shifts the over-lookers would return home to their own beds, whilst the workforce, many of

The Royal & Ancient, Colne Bridge.

whom were children, were locked in the factory overnight.

On one such occasion, a boy named James Thornton was sent to the carding room to fetch roving, equipped with the naked flame of a candle rather than the glass lantern expressly provided for this purpose. Tragically, the boy dropped the candle, which ignited a pile of nearby cotton, and due to the great quantity of combustible material at the factory, the blaze quickly developed into an inferno.

Finding all the doors locked, some of those inside managed to escape by means of ladders but others succumbed to the smoke and confusion. Of the twenty-six people working at Atkinson's mill that night, only nine survived. The remaining seventeen – all girls between the ages of nine and eighteen – perished in the conflagration.

When the fire had finally died out, their bodies were recovered and taken to an impromptu mortuary in the cellar of the Spinners Arms. A newspaper at the time recorded that the corpses were 'in so mutilated a state as to render it impossible for their nearest friends to recognise them'. The children were subsequently laid to rest in the churchyard of St John's at Kirkheaton, where a monument still commemorates the tragedy.

Nine days after the fire, Sir Robert Peel the Elder introduced the Cotton Mills and Factories Act in the House of Commons, which forbade night-time working at such enterprises and restricted the number of hours children could labour. He expressly stated that he hoped the Act would prevent such tragedies from happening again.

Considering the morbid history of the site, it is scarcely any wonder that the Royal

& Ancient has attracted talk of the super-natural. In recent years, the establishment has been bedevilled by poltergeist-type activity. Glasses have been thrown across the bar without any apparent agency and there have been plagues of blowing light bulbs that seemed to go far beyond a mere electrical fault.

Landlady Kelly Routledge told the *Huddersfield Daily Examiner*:

> There's something about the cellar. It's nothing good or bad but I always get the feeling that there's somebody there watching me. The old landlord told us about a spot in the hallway where his dog would just sit and bark when nothing was there. In the store, things have moved to a different place and I was talking to a member of staff one night after the pub closed and she froze and said she could see a lady.

Customers have also witnessed uncanny phenomena at the pub, with several claiming to have seen the figure of a girl wandering around the upper rooms of the building. However, it is perhaps harder to take seriously the account of one patron, who professed to have been trapped in a cubicle in the ladies' toilets by a 'mysterious force', arguably an all too common experience in such establishments!

Meanwhile, paranormal investigators have descended on the Royal & Ancient in force over the last decade and one participant claims to have been scratched on the back of the neck by an invisible entity during such a survey. Despite these tangible manifestations, the latest team to have visited the pub have not reached any firm conclusions and intend to conduct further vigils there in the future.

The White Cross Inn, Bradley

Named after a boundary cross erected by the Cistercian monks of Fountains Abbey in the twelfth century, to mark their lands at Bradley, the White Cross Inn is thought to be one of the oldest hostelries in the Huddersfield region. Although it cannot claim a provenance as ancient as its name, the pub has served alcohol continually under that moniker since the eighteenth century at least. Yet perhaps surprisingly, the ghost that haunts the establishment is thought to be the spirit of an individual who died within living memory.

The spectre is certainly familiar with modern plumbing. During the 1990s, one of the most regular disturbances experienced by landlady Elaine Armer was the sound of footsteps padding along the corridor towards the lavatories in the dead of night, followed by the sound of a flushing toilet. On several occasions, Mrs Armer rose from her bed to search for the intruder, only to find herself the sole person awake in the pub and the curious evidence of a toilet cistern slowly refilling.

Indeed, the spirit seems to have been obsessed with liquids. Puddles of mild bitter were discovered in the middle of the floor on a morning, although both the brewery and a plumber confirmed the pumps were functioning perfectly. Meanwhile, Mrs Armer's daughter, Lynn, was foiled in her attempts to go to bed one night when she discovered her mattress saturated with icy water, despite there being no obvious leak.

The apparition was only occasionally seen; landlord Bill Armer thought he saw a figure enter the toilets one night after time had been called, whilst a family friend caught sight of the reflection of a man in the mirror but could not see any physical source. A local also witnessed the ghost and

The White Cross, Bradley.

felt sure he resembled a former landlord who had died on the premises not too many years earlier. This particularly spooked the regulars who could remember his tenure, and many subsequently refused to use the toilets he was believed to frequent.

The Armer family were eventually forced to appoint a medium who had previously investigated phenomena at the famously haunted Three Nuns pub near Mirfield. She agreed with the identification of the spirit as the deceased landlord and suggested he was searching for his wife, who had since left the pub for a nursing home. The medium duly performed an exorcism and no further trouble was recorded at the White Cross.

Newhouse Hall, Sheepridge

Incongruous amidst the modern housing estates of Brackenhall and Deighton, this brooding sixteenth-century pile is one of the most venerable buildings in the Huddersfield district and equally one of the most romanticised. Over the centuries it has accrued tales of grisly murders, religious persecution, hidden treasure and secret tunnels, not to mention its fair share of spectres.

These apparitions seem to have predominantly troubled the upper floor of the hall. For instance, in one reputedly haunted bedroom, it was said that anybody who slept on a particular bed in the room would awake in the night with the unpleasant awareness of a heavy weight pressing down upon them, like some animal crouching on their chest.

The sensation was attributed to a ghostly dog, which would afterwards disappear into the wall. However, the experience is familiar from supernatural traditions across the world and is often described as being 'hag-ridden'. It is the subject of Henry Fuseli's famous 1782 painting 'The Nightmare', and today it is regarded as nothing more than a distressing occasional symptom of sleep-paralysis.

Newhouse Hall, Sheepridge.

Nonetheless, more tangible nocturnal visitants were in no short supply at Newhouse. An elderly woman who had lived at the hall in the 1870s told local historian Philip Ahier that, whilst staying overnight at the hall, her sister would sporadically scream at an invisible hand she claimed to feel snatching at her.

Meanwhile, maids working there during the mid-nineteenth century frequently complained of witnessing the apparition of a finely-dressed lady pacing the upper corridors at night, and one girl who had served at the hall for thirteen years swore she was often kept awake by the rustle of a silk dress outside her door.

A similar phantom lady was seen in late 1936 on Wiggan Lane adjacent to the hall. Mrs M. Hall of nearby Fartown was returning from a visit to Newhouse late one night, accompanied by her mother. Suddenly up ahead they saw a young woman dressed in white and wearing a flowing veil. This figure then proceeded to float across the road and disappear into an abutting field wall.

Mrs Hall told Terence Whitaker in 1983, 'We took a tighter grip on each other and, picking up courage, looked over the wall into the field, but no one was there. I firmly believe we had seen the ghost of the young woman who is said to haunt the hall.'

Star-Cross'd Lovers

Many of the disturbances at Newhouse Hall are believed to stem from an episode during the English Civil Wars (1642–48) when the hall was home to a renowned beauty by the name of Sybil Brooke. Miss

Brooke attracted countless suitors from across the area but she most favoured a gallant Royalist who dwelled at Toothill Hall, only a short mile away over the crest of the hill towards Brighouse.

Sadly for the young lovers, Sybil's father vehemently opposed the match, despite similarly favouring the Royalist cause. Such was his disapproval, he forbade the couple from meeting, refusing to allow the young cavalier within sight of the hall and confining his daughter to its precincts.

Undeterred, the Toothill lover hit upon a novel scheme by which he could continue to communicate with the object of his affections. This gentleman possessed a faithful and unusually intelligent hound, to whose neck he would attach letters for his beloved. The dog would then bound through Felgreave Wood to Newhouse and deliver the missive to Miss Brooke, who would be waiting patiently at the kitchen window of the hall with a letter of her own for the creature to return.

By some means, however, her father learned of their ruse and one moonlit autumn night when the hound arrived at the kitchen window, it was not Sybil Brooke who received him. Instead, there was the enraged Newhouse patriarch, armed with a sword. With a single blow, he severed the dog's head from its body, slicing the offending letter asunder in the process.

According to tradition, the poor animal remained loyal in its death throes and dutifully sped back to Toothill Hall, albeit with no message other than that signified by the raw stump where its head once sat. The dog's master was supposedly so angered by the terrible injury meted out to his trusty companion that he switched his allegiance to the Roundheads in protest.

Subsequently, Sybil Brooke, distressed by the brutal killing of the hound and the loss of the connection to her lover, began to pine away. She took to wandering listlessly up and down the corridors of the hall until she finally expired from grief.

Hence, tradition holds it to be the restless spirit of Sybil Brooke that has so troubled occupants of Newhouse over the years, pacing the passageways as she had during the last stage of her short life. But whilst the prominent Brooke family undoubtedly resided at Newhouse Hall during the mid-seventeenth century, regrettably there seems to be no evidence to confirm the truth of the story.

Heads or Tails

More gruesomely, the apparition of the mistreated dog is rumoured to haunt the vicinity of Newhouse Hall. On moonlit autumn nights, a headless hound can be seen springing along Wiggan Lane and through Felgreave Wood, retracing the familiar journey back to Toothill Hall. The tale is often accompanied by the warning, 'Whoever sees this dog, misfortune shall befall'.

Curiously, another phantom canine is supposed to prowl through the trees of Felgreave Wood and it is difficult to decide which potential encounter would be more distressing. For not only does this dog still possess a head, it is apparently a human head with 'a beard stretching from ear to ear'.

During the mid-nineteenth century, this bizarre monstrosity was witnessed by a local woman named Elizabeth Haigh, who was so unnerved by the sight she fell into a faint and was discovered the following day still unconscious. Some hundred years later, Philip Ahier spoke to at least two people who claimed to have seen the beast, one of whom reported that as soon as he let his

Felgreave Wood, Sheepridge – haunted by a ghostly hound?.

eyes wander from the spectacle, it vanished into thin air.

Nonetheless, Ahier believed that a prosaic explanation could be found to account for the manifestation. During the eighteenth century, Felgreave Wood was noted for its game, especially pheasants and hare, and so Ahier surmised that tales of the ghost had originally been spread by gamekeepers to deter poachers. To reinforce the legend, one of the keepers would periodically dress in furs and crawl through the wood, making sure he was observed by some credulous witness!

It seems unlikely that the phantom dog reputed to disturb sleepers in that bedroom at Newhouse Hall is associated with the hound belonging to the Toothill cavalier or indeed the bearded grotesque of Felgreave Wood. This dog is too at home at Newhouse. Nonetheless, it is intriguing that there are quite so many tales concerning such spectres in that neighbourhood.

It may be that the stories are actually all variations on a much older supernatural tradition. Phantom dogs have been feared in Western Europe since the ninth century at least and are a familiar trope in British ghost lore. Depending on the region, such apparitions are variously known as a bar-guest, guytrash, skriker, padfoot or old shuck. They are reputed to betide ill-fortune to anybody who sees them, much like the headless hound of Felgreave Wood.

As such, a phantom dog may have haunted the environs of Sheepridge for many centuries before the English Civil War. The story of Sybil Brooke and the Toothill hound might simply represent a picturesque narrative added in later years to account for the origin of the apparition. Nonetheless, with sightings persisting well into the twentieth century, we should perhaps be careful before we write it off as mere folklore.

Fixby Hall

Like so many grand houses around Huddersfield today, Fixby Hall is probably better known for its thriving golf club than any ancestral spectres that may still be clinging on in the face of modernity. Nonetheless, the hall is the perfect setting for such supernatural encounters. Its origins are shrouded in mystery; a manor house seems to have existed at the site in the Middle Ages and the structure of the building standing today probably dates back to the sixteenth century, albeit substantially altered during the Georgian period.

The hall may also have played a role on the fringes of a couple of turbulent episodes in English history. One long-established family in the region maintained an apocryphal tradition that Bonnie Prince Charlie briefly lodged there in early 1746 as he retreated from Derby back to Scotland, following the defeat of the Jacobite Rebellion. After passing a night within the safety of its walls and commandeering the contents of the cellar, he torched the building and continued on his way.

Then, during the early decades of the nineteenth century, the house was tenanted by the renowned social reformer Sir Richard Oastler. Despite Oastler's tireless work in improving working conditions, his landlord, Thomas Thornhill, was a hated man locally and in 1811 Luddites mounted an attack on Fixby Hall whilst Oastler was in residence. The assault resulted in a small skirmish in the grounds, fought largely with pitchforks and sticks. Oastler himself was later evicted from the hall by Thornhill and placed in a debtors' prison after his philanthropy led him into financial difficulties.

Any of these events could account for the horde of riches supposedly stashed at Fixby Hall and its supernatural attendant. The story was originally brought before a baffled session of the West Riding Court in 1881, when a mother and daughter attempted to apply for a warrant permitting them to search the house and grounds for the hidden wealth, to which they believed they were entitled.

The daughter explained that she had lately been visited at night by an apparition

Fixby Hall.

wearing a grey coat, with watery blue eyes. This ghost had informed the girl that one of her ancestors had come to an untimely end at Fixby Hall and been buried in the cellars, accompanied by a great sum of money and a will. Unsurprisingly, the judge refused the request but in subsequent years, a phantom fitting the same description was observed walking through the cellars at the hall, perhaps condemned by the court's decision to go on protecting his secret legacy until one of his heirs is finally able to claim it.

The Grey Horse Inn, Birchencliffe

When Richard Lloyd took over the license of the Grey Horse Inn during the summer of 2007, he soon discovered that he had acquired more than he'd bargained for. Perhaps a new landlord would treat his bar staff's refusal to enter the cellar with a degree of suspicion, but following a series of inexplicable events Mr Lloyd was forced to accept that something strange was happening in his pub.

The Grey Horse Inn, Birchencliffe.

His own first encounter with the phenomena occurred whilst he was drinking at the bar with a couple of regulars and suddenly a wine glass 'shattered violently' on the shelf without any obvious cause. Meanwhile, he began to find gas cylinders in the cellar mysteriously turned-off, often with such force that the knobs had jammed – a feat of strength Mr Lloyd considered beyond any of his employees.

Indeed, most of the disturbances were concentrated in the cellar, which was notorious for its unnaturally cold atmosphere and flickering lights. Barmaid Hayley Dart refused to descend at all, and even Mr Lloyd was forced to admit that it possessed an uncanny atmosphere: 'I've been down there and the hairs on the back of your neck stand up. It doesn't feel right and I'm the most cynical and sceptical person.'

In addition to the poltergeist activity, the landlord soon heard tales of a former proprietor who had seen a spectral figure emerge from the cellar some time in the 1990s. Yet the Grey Horse does not have a particularly ancient or colourful history to account for such manifestations. It was rumoured that somebody committed suicide on the premises in the mid-twentieth century, but such stories are suspiciously common and often apocryphal.

One fact may be significant, however. The pub had originally been converted from cottages in the 1860s and, during renovations some 120 years later, workmen discovered the building had been constructed over an old well, around 20 feet in depth.

Wells are a recurrent motif in haunted house lore, both in narrative and explanatory terms. Harry Price famously discovered several wells in the cellars of Borley Rectory, once styled 'the most haunted house in the world', whilst literary supernaturalists have not failed to exploit the atmospheric potential of such features – at least two classic ghost stories by M.R. James revolve around abandoned wells.

Although there is a primal superstition that disturbing an old well can release things best left forgotten, sceptical voices have also considered the implication of wells. G.W. Lambert, President of the Society for Psychical Research, first suggested that underground water sources might be responsible for hauntings in 1955, arguing that they could cause structural disturbances mistaken for poltergeist activity.

Whilst Lambert's original hypothesis has been disproved (as vibrations of the necessary magnitude would shake the house apart), it was later modified to incorporate Vic Tandy's suggestion that many hauntings are associated with low-frequency soundwaves, potentially generated by underground water sources. In the context of the Grey Horse, it seems appropriate that Tandy's research was published under the title, 'Something in the Cellar'.

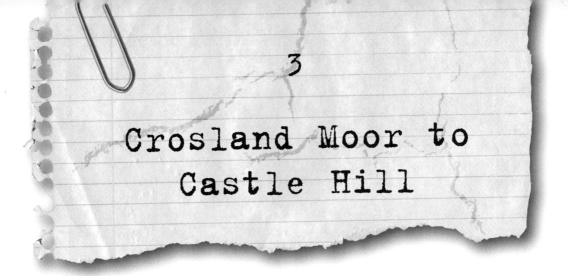

3
Crosland Moor to Castle Hill

The Dalton Triangle

An unassuming suburb of Huddersfield just over a mile from the town centre, Dalton was once a notable settlement in its own right, mentioned in the Domesday Book of 1086. However, it was not until the Industrial Revolution that the community grew to any significance size. During this period, the area became strongly associated with the wealthy Tolson family, and their legacy to the town, the Tolson Museum at Ravensknowle Hall, is arguably Dalton's most celebrated feature today.

Curiously, it is also one of Huddersfield's most haunted districts, with a number of stories stemming from a very specific area around Dalton Green Lane and Greenhead Lane. Sadly, several of the buildings in question have now been demolished to make way for the modern housing estates that now dominate the area. However, such was the strength of the original manifestations, it would not be surprising to find that their uncanny influence lives on, even after the structures themselves are forgotten.

Dives House

Once known locally as 'The Old Bogard', in reference to its haunted reputation ('bogard' or 'boggart' being an archaic dialect word for a type of ghost), Dives House formerly stood near the junction of Wakefield Road and Dalton Green Lane. The rambling homestead was demolished in the mid-1950s after falling into a state of irreparable dereliction; however, its destruction was widely regarded as a sad loss, for the history of Dives House was illustrious to say the least.

It is not known precisely when the house had originally been built – possibly as early as the fourteenth century – but by the time of the Dissolution of the Monasteries in the 1530s, it belonged to a stubbornly Catholic family known as the Langleys. Until he sold it in 1567, it was home to Richard Langley II, who persistently declined to recognise the strictures of the Reformation.

Langley refused to subscribe to the Act of Supremacy, which named Elizabeth I the ecclesiastical authority in England, and as a result he was executed in 1586. Like so many convicted of high treason, he was hanged, drawn and quartered, whilst his mortal remains were denied a Christian burial. Several centuries later, in 1929, Pope Pius XI beatified Langley as a Catholic martyr.

Not only had Langley refused to renounce his own faith, he had been instrumental in protecting the faith of others. It is certain that he gave refuge to Catholic priests at his Grimthorpe and Ousethorpe properties, and a persistent tradition in Dalton held that he hid them at Dives House. Although no documentary confirmation has been discovered, renovation work during the early twentieth century revealed two concealed rooms which could well have been used as priest-holes.

A related legend claims that Dives House was occupied by three Catholic priests for a period during the post-Reformation persecutions. One night a quarrel over theological matters got out of hand and one priest killed his brother, who was then secretly buried beneath the lawn. Some historians have suggested that even if this narrative is false, it may represent a corrupted remembrance of a time when Catholic priests were indeed covertly interred at Dives House, as they would have been denied burial in a Protestant churchyard.

With so much tragedy connected to Dives House, it is scarcely surprising that it gained a sinister reputation in later centuries. Mysterious footsteps were frequently heard on the main staircase and in the cellars, especially around the change of the new moon. On one occasion, the occupants of the house were roused in the night by their Airedale dog barking furiously, as if at an intruder. After silencing the dog, they grew aware of the sound of feet on the stairs but despite a thorough search of the house, no trespasser was found.

One particular bedchamber was regarded with especial dread. Those who slept in the room claimed to have been troubled by a 'mysterious eerie presence' and an unearthly ball of light which travelled along the wall and disappeared at the top of the landing. This spectacle was witnessed on several occasions and seemed to occur even when the room was completely shuttered, precluding any external source for the illumination.

Meanwhile, one individual maintained he'd seen the apparition of a tall lady wearing a black dress and white apron at the foot of the bed; another claimed that all the sheets had been torn from the bed in the middle of the night. Such disturbances were supposed to be at their strongest on 15 November, although if this date has any historical significance, it remains unclear.

Mill Hill Hospital

Mill Hill House was originally occupied by the Tolson family when they first settled in Dalton in 1840. The patriarch, James Tolson, established a textiles industry in the village which, only ten years later, employed over 700 people. The Tolsons heirs eventually vacated Mill Hill House for their own, newly-built mansions nearby and Mill Hill House was purchased clandestinely by the Huddersfield Corporation, as the potential site for a new smallpox hospital.

Inevitably, local opposition was strong, but a temporary sanatorium was opened at Mill Hill in 1893, followed by the construction of a dedicated hospital for the treatment of infectious diseases in 1898. It primarily operated as a fever hospital until 1968, when the vaccination programme had all but eradicated such viruses in Britain. The institution was then used for geriatric patients and administration until 1997, when the building was demolished and the site sold for new housing.

In April 1964, the night shift at Mill Hill Hospital was disrupted by an outbreak of uncanny activity on one of the wards. Over a dozen nurses complained about doors and windows opening and closing of their own accord, and a mysterious wailing sound ripping through the air. There were even rumours that an unspecified apparition had been seen to materialise. The patients and day-shift staff were unaffected, but several nurses refused to undertake night duty until the disturbances had been investigated.

In an attempt to convince the nurses there was nothing to be afraid of, hospital officials agreed to observe the allegedly haunted ward overnight. A sceptical spokesman for the management said, 'There is no doubt that the nurses are genuinely frightened but these scares are an occupational disease among nurses who work at night on quiet wards.' Unsurprisingly, these clumsy conciliatory gestures failed to resolve the situation and finally the hospital chaplain had to be called to conduct a blessing ceremony in the ward.

Oaklands

The fine mansion known as Oaklands was built for Robert Tolson in 1850 and originally stood amidst 3 acres of landscaped parkland. During the Second World War, it was used to accommodate evacuated children and in 1944 was purchased outright by the Huddersfield Corporation, which deployed it as a nursing home for many years. The building is now a Learning and Development Centre for Kirklees Council, whilst the surrounding parkland has been entirely consumed by modern housing.

In 1965, the matron, Gwynneth Jardine, witnessed the apparition of a 'tall military looking gentleman with a long white beard' in her room one night. Several days later, she read in the newspaper that Muriel Tolson, last of that distinguished family, had passed away in Harrogate at around the same time as her mysterious encounter. Mrs Jardine also subsequently discovered from a portrait in the Tolson Museum that the figure she'd seen bore a striking resemblance to Whiteley Tolson, who had resided at Oaklands until his death in 1928.

This type of 'crisis apparition' is a common feature of British ghost lore and many august dynasties have traditions to the effect that the wraith of an ancestor appears when a death in the family is about to occur. Whiteley Tolson certainly had good reason to mourn the passing of his line; his own two sons were killed in action in the First World War, a tragedy that led their uncle, Legh Tolson, to donate Ravensknowle Hall to the town in their memory, itself leading to the establishment of the Tolson Museum.

Oakland's old lodge house was also the scene of supernatural activity around the same time. The building has now been demolished, but in the early 1960s it was a private residence occupied by Susan Richardson and her family. Several times she saw the figure of a young girl staring at her through the window – the child then proceeded to walk away and disappear. The sighting was corroborated by a friend on a separate occasion and an elderly neighbour told her that a nine-year-old girl had once died in the house.

Mrs Richardson also heard the sound of horses' hooves coming from the empty stable block, mysterious footsteps, and a woman's voice whispering with urgency. Shortly before the family moved out of the lodge, due in part to these occurrences, Susan told the *Huddersfield Daily Examiner*, 'When we moved into the house I felt that it

Oaklands, Dalton.

was a happy atmosphere, but toward the end of our stay I felt something had changed... and we were no longer welcome.'

Woodsome, Fenay Bridge

One of the most venerable buildings in the Huddersfield district, the current Woodsome Hall, was built in 1517 by the Kay family, who had owned land in the area since the fourteenth century at least. It later passed by marriage into the hands of the Earls of Dartmouth and, in 1921,

became home to the Woodsome Hall Golf Club, who still occupy the site today. It was also once considered the abode of Huddersfield's most notorious spectre, the revenant of a former estate steward by the name of Rimmington.

A room in the hall known as Rimmington's Closet (now the ladies' locker room) was regarded as his favoured haunt owing to the unearthly noises frequently heard emanating from within. The apparition was also frequently seen beyond the confines of the old house, often on horseback, galloping down Woodsome

Woodsome Lane, Fenay Bridge.

Lane with a pack of hunting dogs following in his wake. On one occasion, a witness reported seeing the ghost pluck a brag-nail from the doorpost of a house in the nearby village of Farnley Tyas, although no explanation for this peculiar behaviour has ever been offered.

It is said that Rimmington's spirit became such a nuisance to the occupants of Woodsome Hall that a local clergyman had to be summoned to exorcise the unwelcome presence. The priest performed the necessary rituals, laying the ghost in a grove of beech trees in the grounds of the hall. However, Rimmington avoided his fate by transforming into a robin and so continued to visit Woodsome with impunity, although presumably this manifestation was regarded as less of an irritation.

Belief in Rimmington's ghost was first recorded in 1868 by the seminal Huddersfield historian, Charles Hobkirk, who expressed bafflement at the existence of such a tradition. Rimmington had been steward to the Kay family in the late seventeenth century – his death is recorded in 1696 – and by all accounts he was a pious man who dealt fairly with the estate tenants and enjoyed the friendship of the local clergy. There seems to be no obvious biographical reason why his restless spirit should continue to walk.

Hobkirk dismissed the belief as vulgar superstition, whilst another local historian has wondered if the tradition might 'have its origins in some long forgotten and probably clandestine act', with reference to the ghost's peculiar behaviour in Farnley Tyas. It is certainly possible that this is a symbolic narrative, designed to encode transgressive activity – folklore often fulfils such a function. However, it transpires that Rimmington's spectre is not confined to the imagination of nineteenth-century rustics.

A more recent sighting of the phantom occurred in 1991, when a driver joining Woodsome Lane from the direction of Almondbury was forced to swerve violently to avoid a collision with a man on horseback who suddenly appeared from a gap in an adjacent wall, accompanied by several dogs. Yet a passenger in the car denied seeing any such figure and when the driver looked back, there was no evidence to the contrary. More puzzlingly still, when the driver returned to the spot the following day in an attempt to explain his encounter, he could find no gate or track from which a rider could have emerged.

Castle Hill

Rising almost 1,000 feet above the town and crowned by Victoria Tower, Castle Hill is undoubtedly Huddersfield's most prominent landmark. The tower itself was built between 1897 and 1899 to commemorate Queen Victoria's Diamond Jubilee, but even prior to the folly's construction, the summit had long been exploited for a variety of purposes. Over the millennia the hill has been home to prehistoric hunter-gatherers, an Iron Age hill-fort, a Norman motte-and-bailey, a fourteenth-century village, an Armada beacon, Chartist rallies, bare-knuckle boxing, cockfights, a bowling green and, until quite recently, a public house.

Understandably, such a significant landscape feature has accrued its fair share of folklore. Stories go that the hill is the abode of a fearsome dragon, guarding its golden horde, or that the Devil himself wanders a labyrinth of secret tunnels beneath the summit, having leapt there from Scar Top at Netherton, a couple of miles away. Castle Hill has also been suggested as one of the strongholds of Cartimandua, Queen of the Brigantes, and even the location for King Arthur's mythical fortress, Camelot.

The Almondbury Padfoot

Whilst these tales are the most commonly related legends pertaining to Castle Hill, it is not clear to what extent they were genuinely regarded as 'true' by the local populace, even when they were collected in previous centuries. However, they have often been discussed at the expense of a less grandiose but apparently more sincere supernatural belief recorded in the 1800s – a belief which relates not so much to the summit of the hill itself but to the patchwork of hamlets, lanes and woodland dappling its flanks.

These places were once known as haunts of the padfoot, a spectral hound that stalked anybody unfortunate enough to be abroad in the neighbourhood at night. As discussed previously in relation to Newhouse Hall, these phantom dogs were once familiar throughout Britain and went by a variety of local names. In earlier periods, they were generally regarded as demons in corporeal form, rather than ghosts, sometimes shape-shifters, adopting a variety of guises from a cow to a rolling woolsack. They tended to lurk at liminal locations such as highways, bridges or parish boundaries and were essentially the guardian spirit of these places.

By the nineteenth century, their form was primarily that of a ghostly dog, albeit one of unusual stature, with flaming eyes. In some cases, an explanatory narrative was concocted and attached to the beast to account for its presence – such may have

Castle Hill, Almondbury.

All Hallows' Church, Almondbury.

been the case with the headless hound of Newhouse Hall and Felgreave Wood. The padfoot that haunted the environs of Almondbury and Castle Hill was a more ambiguous manifestation, but nonetheless its existence seems to have been widely believed and feared in the district, whilst several correspondents of the antiquarian, Reverend Alfred Easther, even claimed to have encountered it.

The Almondbury Padfoot was typically described as a grey or white hound, almost the size of a bear, with 'eyes as big as tea-plates'. It was known to menace locals out-and-about on nocturnal errands and to witness the fiend was often regarded as a portent of death or disaster. Not everybody seems to have been able to see it. One local woman found herself transfixed by the padfoot's stare through her window one night; inquiring what the matter was, her sister came over to the pane but denied that she could distinguish anything untoward. However, as soon as she took her mesmerised sister's hand, it appeared to her.

Curious Incidents of the Dog in the Night Time

Reverend Easther relates the story of a man he refers to as Old A.M., who encountered the padfoot one night as he returned to his home at Upper Fold after buying milk and butter at Royd House. The gigantic hound appeared before him on Sharp Lane and although Old A.M. demanded, 'What wantest thou wi' me?' the thing just stared malevolently at him. Old A.M. set off walking again with his pail of milk, but the padfoot transformed into a calf and pursued him all the way home. As he reached his own door, a paralysis seized him and he found himself unable to turn the handle.

Fortunately, his wife opened it before the padfoot could claim him.

The following evening, Old A.M. was enjoying the company of some friends at a cottage at Sharp Lane end. He refused to travel home alone on account of his experience the previous night. Another present by the name of Old Joe North mocked his conviction and determined to return home in solitude. However, it was not long before the phantom dog confronted him. He tried to shoo it but it turned again into a calf and passed through a number of different forms as it tracked him. Old Joe thought he would outwit it by passing through the yard of All Hallows' Church, but he found it waiting for him at the other end and he only just made it home.

Around 1820, another individual who lived at Farnley Bank encountered the padfoot whilst on his way to consult a doctor in Almondbury village. It followed him most of the way, making a sound like 'shog, shog, shog' until he lost it in the vicinity of the church. However, as he left the doctor's it leapt out at him from a nearby alley and trailed him as far as Shrogg Wood. Meanwhile, a man named Joe B. claimed to have been physically assaulted by the padfoot on Thorpe Lane in the centre of Almondbury, and Johnny B. often found his way obstructed by the beast on Clough Hall Lane, which encircles the summit of Castle Hill.

Dog Days are Over?

Speaking to Almondbury locals in 1883, Reverend Easther found that the majority of folk believed the padfoot no longer haunted the neighbourhood. The advent of industry, higher populations and modern farming techniques had largely destroyed

the lonely places in which it thrived. Yet as recently as 1965, Susan Richardson told the *Huddersfield Daily Examiner* that Sharp Lane and the fields between the summit of Castle Hill and Molly Carr Wood were home to 'hostile' apparitions. Perhaps whilst the black dog archetype has passed from the collective psyche, the phenomena that produced such sightings linger on.

Stephen Wade has collected a couple of more recent sightings of phantom dogs elsewhere in the Huddersfield region. He records a belief amongst poachers on Saddleworth Moor that the remote plateau was haunted by a spectral hound 'the size of a hoss', with piercing red eyes. Wade also relates the story of a man walking home from Lindley to Paddock late one night, when he heard a howl behind him 'like you imagine from *The Hound of the Baskervilles*'. Turning to scrutinise the darkness, he saw the silhouette of a large, amorphous shape, with the gait of a cat but the profile of a dog, sloping off into the gloom.

Longley Old Hall, Longley

Whilst there has been a hall at Longley since the fourteenth century at least, it rose to significance around 1531 when it was acquired by the Ramsden family, Lords of the Manor of Huddersfield and Almondbury. Such was the Ramsden's association with Longley, they retained the hall as their base in the region even after they'd offloaded their estate to the Huddersfield Corporation in 1920. It was not until 1977 that the hall finally passed out of the hands of the family.

At least some of the fabric of the current structure dates to the medieval period, but it has been successively altered over the centuries and the building is now a hodge-podge of architectural styles. This variety has proved quite a challenge for its current owners, Robin and Christine Gallagher, in their attempts to restore the hall to its former glory. But whatever the antiquity of its various parts, the house still possesses a brooding, ancient atmosphere and remains the perfect habitat for the ghosts of its illustrious past.

The exact identity of the spirits at Longley Old Hall remains a mystery, although there have been a number of such sightings. Builders engaged in restoration work have reported the figure of a 'woman in a black, flowered gown' on separate occasions, whilst another claims to have regularly witnessed 'a boy in breeches and a ruffled shirt' watching him from the garden.

In recent years, the hall has been open to the public by appointment. Speaking to the *Huddersfield Daily Examiner*, Robin Gallagher commented, 'When people come to visit, the most frequently asked question is "Have you any ghosts?" We don't tell them there and then, but ask them to guess which rooms have a "presence". More often than not, someone gets it right.' This suggests that even if a supernatural hypothesis is rejected, there may be some objective, atmospheric component that produces these impressions.

Longley Old Hall, Longley – home to a number of spectres.

Deadmanstone, Berry Brow

Students of toponymy cannot help but be intrigued by the incongruous name of this residential street in the Holme Valley village of Berry Brow. It is the sort of title you might expect to find in a Gothic novel rather than the extensively redeveloped suburb of a West Yorkshire milltown. Yet the area can boast enough macabre traditions and attendant spooks to justify its sinister nomenclature, and whilst the memory of much of this lore may be dying out, certain phenomena seem to endure.

In recent years one particular cottage, which backs on to Deadmanstone, has gained a reputation for being difficult to let, and those who do take the lease rarely stay for long. One tenant was forced to leave the house following a series of terrifying incidents, which began with the sound of whispering voices emanating from within the house whenever he placed his key in the front door lock. Soon, he began to complain of a hostile presence at the top of the stairs and one night he was woken by an invisible force shaking him ferociously. Following this, he started sleeping downstairs but the presence pursued him.

A friend who stayed in the house also experienced strange phenomena on several occasions, such as the sound of murmuring voices and a threatening atmosphere at the top of the stairs. Moreover, this friend claimed to have witnessed apparitions in the building when he awoke in the middle of the night. They took the form of a tall, thin man wearing black and a small

Deadmanstone, Berry Brow.

girl bouncing a ball. Both appeared to be dressed in the style of the seventeenth or eighteenth century.

The site of the street today was originally occupied by Deadmanstone House, a Georgian mansion built to replace an earlier medieval fortified manor. This grand edifice was demolished in the 1960s – along with a great number of other buildings in Berry Brow – but a decade later a local clergyman writing on the subject of the village's history recalled that an unspecified ghost had once been reputed to wander the corridors of Deadmanstone House.

Most historians now agree that the name 'Deadmanstone' refers to the land itself – a corruption the Old English 'Dudman's tun',

meaning 'the farm belonging to Dudman'. However, local folklore has preserved a few more colourful explanations to account for the unusual name and whilst it is difficult to confirm the veracity of these traditions one way or another, if either legend is true it may explain why the area has been so plagued by uncanny phenomena over the years.

The first tale claims that a couple of centuries ago, the skeleton of a soldier, still wearing his full regalia, was discovered sealed in a small natural cave in one of the gritstone outcrops in the grounds of the house. In some versions, the soldier is a Roman centurion; in others he is Scottish warrior, possibly a relic of Edward Bruce's border raids during the thirteenth century. The stories relate that he was presumed to have been a sentry caught napping and, as punishment, was walled-up in the cave and left to die a particularly unpleasant death. However, it is important to note that no physical or documentary evidence of this discovery has been preserved and the tale may be entirely apocryphal.

A second tradition claims that the name 'Deadmanstone' derives from a curious gritstone boulder which can still be seen today. A natural passage has been weathered through the base of the rock, just large enough to allow a person to squeeze from one side to the other. In the 1950s, after the hollow had been cleared following many years choked with debris, it was customary for children to play a game in which one of their number laid stiff and the others had to pass their friend's supine body through the hole in the stone.

The explanation given for this strange custom is that the rock had once been a station where pallbearers rested the coffin on a corpse-route between villages such as Meltham or South Crosland and the parish church at Almondbury. It was believed that whilst sojourning at the 'Dead Man's Stone', the pallbearers would remove the body from its coffin and pass it through the fissure in the rock, before replacing it in the coffin and continuing with their journey. The children played their game in imitation of this alleged practice.

Such a tradition is unlikely to be true in itself, but it is worth noting that holed stones were often a source of fascination to the pre-modern mind. Portable examples were known as 'hag stones' and used as protection against witches, whilst larger examples such as Men-an-Tol in Cornwall or Ponden Kirk near Haworth were believed to bestow good health or mar-riage respectively on anybody who passed through their natural portals. Consequently, whilst the name 'Deadmanstone' may not derive from the morbid tradition described above, the stone could still have been associated with ritual use for many centuries.

Coppice Drive, Netherton

Whilst hauntings are typically associated with sites of some antiquity, a number have also been experienced in modern houses without any recorded history of tragedy. Such was the case at a house in Coppice Drive in Netherton, which had only been built in the 1970s on a site that had previously been used as farmland. Yet in 1999, the Barsby family — especially their three-year-old child, Luke — were terrorised by a manifestation reminiscent of something from the BBC's infamous 1993 Halloween drama, *Ghostwatch*.

Luke's mother, Stacey Barsby, told the *Huddersfield Daily Examiner* that her son would no longer be left alone in his bedroom to play with his toys; this was because of the presence of a 'diseased' figure lurking in one corner. Mrs Barsby explained, 'Luke started saying there was a man in the room and could I make the man better. Last Sunday Luke was sobbing hysterically, saying "Please don't put me in the bedroom, that man's coming." He was petrified.'

Mrs Barsby herself also heard movements coming from the bedroom when she knew it to be empty, and detected a noticeable chill around the window area, which left icicles hanging from the frame even when the central heating was turned on full. The family dog refused to enter the affected room and would bark furiously in its direction, whilst the cat scratched frantically at the door to escape when it got shut in.

Coppice Drive, Netherton.

At their wit's end, the Barsbys called in the vicar from Holy Trinity Church, South Crosland, who had baptised the infant Luke. The priest visited the house, blessing both the building and the child. However, whilst Luke was able to fall asleep happily that night, he woke in the early hours of the morning, screaming 'He's back!' The family went on to consult the diocese Deliverance Minister (the name by which the Church of England now refers to members of the clergy trained to performed exorcisms) but the outcome is not recorded.

Ultimately, the family felt the issue had been resolved by the intervention of spiritualist medium Rita Littlewood. She claimed to have detected the spirit of an elderly man who had died in Luke's bedroom following a lengthy illness, and helped him to pass on. How this fits with the documented history of the house – only one previous occupant, who had slept in the other bedroom – is not clear. Nonetheless, the Barsbys were happy with the outcome, reporting that their son now slept in peace.

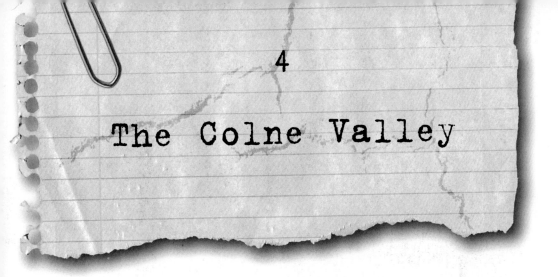

4

The Colne Valley

Milnsbridge House

To see it today, hemmed in on every side by soot-stained Victorian terraces, it is difficult to imagine that Milnsbridge House was formerly a grand country residence set amongst spacious and verdant grounds. Indeed, following its construction in 1756 and for many decades thereafter, this palatial, three-storey residence with its imposing Classical façade was the jewel in Colne Valley's crown. Peacocks wandered its rolling lawns; swans flocked around an ornamental pond; peaches and nectarines grew in abundance on the trees. As late as 1829, one visitor described its situation as 'of the most fertile and beautiful description'.

However, as the nineteenth century wore on and industry increasingly defaced the valley, the fortunes of Milnsbridge House began to wane. By 1901, it had been divided into five separate residences, the gardens sold off and built over. Then, in 1923, it was purchased by metal-merchants W.H. Robinson Ltd, who gutted the interior for conversion into industrial units. Although the building has since been listed, this is the state in which it remains today; a shabby husk of its former self, enveloped by the industrial twilight.

In the 1930s, whilst lecturing to the Milnsbridge Naturalist Society, local historian Philip Ahier was told of a tradition that Milnsbridge House was haunted by 'the ghost of a tall man dressed in black clothes', although nobody present could provide any more detail. The report was originally treated cursorily, as little more than a nebulous superstition of the sort that attaches itself to many imposing old buildings. But since that time, independent sources have experienced strange phenomena in the vicinity of the house, perhaps giving credence to the information received by Ahier.

One long-standing Milnsbridge resident recalled how as children in the early 1940s, he and friend managed to gain access to the cellars of the house. 'As we cautiously advanced, aided by a candle in a jar, we heard slow moving footsteps on the floor above. Knowing the building was totally deserted one common thought struck us! We scrambled frantically out of the house and ran until we felt safe.' Significantly, the cellar of the house has a thick, brick-vaulted ceiling through which no human footsteps could've been heard.

Milnsbridge House, Milsnbridge.

even held in the cellars at Radcliffe's residence whilst they were interrogated.

Whilst a few Luddites were undoubtedly criminals – such as those who murdered local mill-owner William Horsfall – many others were simply trying to protect their family's livelihood from the dehumanising consequences of mechanisation, at a time when the English economy was already suffering from the Napoleonic Wars. But this brooked no sympathy from Radcliffe. As George Searle Phillips wrote, 'If any insurgents were brought before him, his mercy was law, his justice, execution. As easily might you wring blood out of the obdurate rocks which frowned in shaggy horror over his mansion as compassion out of his iron heart.'

More recently, a teenage boy found himself disturbed by an uncanny encounter whilst walking his dog on the canal bank in the vicinity of Milnsbridge. Dusk was falling and through the deepening twilight he glimpsed a 'tall, black figure in what looked like a long black coat', lingering on a bridge ahead. Suddenly his dog refused to go any further and rising up on its haunches, began to bark furiously at the shadowy form. The lad stopped to tend to the animal but to no avail and when he looked towards the bridge again, there was nobody to be seen.

Such an account might easily be explained away were it not for the figure's remarkable similarity to Ahier's record of the spectre at Milnsbridge House, a record of which the boy had no knowledge. But who might this darkly garbed apparition actually represent? The most likely candidate seems to be Sir Joseph Radcliffe, a tyrannical magistrate who occupied Milnsbridge House between 1795 and 1819. He was responsible for ruthlessly suppressing the Luddite revolt around Huddersfield in 1812 and sent many to the gallows for their involvement, some of whom were

The Golcar Lily

Upon seeing the rows of weavers cottages nestled on steep slopes above the Colne Valley, former Poet Laureate, Sir John Betjeman, is said to have dubbed Golcar 'the Provence of the North'. Residents of the village, all too familiar with its brisk climate, might disagree with that assessment but it is the sort of picturesque image that habitually attaches itself to the settlement. Those same residents are sometimes referred to as 'Golcar Lilies', after the emblem of the town, although the origins of this motif are shrouded in mystery.

One theory holds that before the Industrial Revolution poisoned the local air, lilies grew in great abundance on the hillside, whilst another maintains the bracing air of the village gave its girls a pink and white complexion evocative of a lily. Some more sober historians suggest it was imported with the Huguenots, French Protestants who fled persecution in their native land in the sixteenth century. Many were weaving families, making the Colne Valley an ideal place to settle, perhaps bringing with them their heraldic symbol, the Lily of France.

But despite the putative pedigree of its name, the Golcar Lily pub on Slades Road is not an establishment of any great antiquity. It was built in 1875 as a Co-op grocery store and, following its closure in the mid-twentieth century, it spent some time split into commercial and residential property before being converted into the present hostelry in 1982. Nonetheless, the place is clearly old enough to have acquired a resident ghost, albeit one that is typically felt or heard rather than seen.

Speaking in 1999, landlord Don Grundy said, 'Staff members past and present have reported strange draughts, hearing bumps and mystery hands touching them.' On one occasion, the Colne Valley Male Voice Choir, who rehearse at the pub, sought to invoke the spirit with a performance of Gilbert & Sullivan's 'The Ghost's High Noon', but to no avail. Its reticence has led staff to conclude that it is a friendly spectre, possibly that of Constance Woodhead, an elderly lady who died in her sleep there in 1978.

The Old Golf House Hotel, Outlane

Located barely a hair's breadth from the busy M62 motorway, the Old Golf House Hotel never seems far from the talismanic buzz of modernity. Yet despite this omnipresent thrum, business travellers are not the only guests to have taken up residency at the Outlane establishment: according to its beleaguered staff, other, less welcome visitors stalk the corridors and conference suites. Cold spots blight the fifty-two bedchambers; taps turn themselves on and off in certain bathrooms; mysterious footsteps and the awareness of some lingering presence plague employees as they try to conduct their duties.

A figure has also been seen lingering in the hallways and stairwells, especially on the first floor of the old wing. It has been described as the image of a sombre woman, dressed in a dark-hued Victorian gown and pinafore. One member of staff, watching from outside the hotel, witnessed the form pass by a window within. Yet nothing appeared at the next window, nor did anything pass the first window again, despite there being no other exits from that corridor.

The apparition has also been glimpsed on the kitchen stairs and at the intersection with the modern wing. Housekeeper Wendy Hornes claims, 'I have never seen it but you walk along the hall and feel as if someone's following you. You hear doors go but no one appears.' Despite such disturbances, employees at the Old Golf House remain stoic. Speaking to the *Huddersfield Daily Examiner*, Ms Hornes insisted that 'You get used to it,' while kitchen worker

The Old Golf House Hotel, Outlane – home to a spectral woman dressed in a Victorian gown.

Kathleen Hayes added, 'She has never hurt anyone, so why bother about it?'

Whilst the hotel is not exactly an old structure – despite the seventeenth-century façade, the fabric of the oldest part only dates to 1862 – it has a colourful past none-theless. The site on which it was erected encroaches on the remains of an extensive Roman fort, constructed towards the end of the first century AD and thought to have been a major outpost on an ancient trans-Pennine highway.

More significantly, however, from 1904 to 1928 the building itself was an orphan-age administered by the Huddersfield Poor Law Union. Some such institutions were notorious as little more than workhouses for the young, and who knows what cruel-ties and privations may have been endured by children housed at Outlane? Certainly, staff who have seen the apparition agree that its attire matches that of guardians shown in old photographs of the children's home and so it may be that one warden patrols there still.

Greenfield Lodge, Scammonden

Perched on the moors above Scammonden Water, Greenfield Lodge presents a stark and windswept countenance to the world. Perhaps it is not as remote as it once was – just a few hundred yards away the ver-tiginous Scammonden Bridge carries Saddleworth Road over the M62 as it passes through the deep Deanhead cutting – but it still seems a lonely sort of place. And whilst the washed-out legend 'TEAS' daubed on the east-facing wall of the building testifies to its former life as a roadside café, scant comfort is to be found there today.

Nonetheless, with fifteen rooms, it is a substantial residence and has served a variety of functions over the years. It was originally constructed in the eighteenth century as a shooting lodge, at which time it was known as the Red House. The name was changed to Greenfield Lodge around 1847, when it was extended. Later, the building came into the possession of a charitable religious soci-ety for a period, which put it to use as a holiday home for underprivileged children, utilising the now-derelict barn and stable as dormitories.

Supernatural activity at Greenfield Lodge was first noticed in 1958, shortly after George and Marjorie Bryant had taken occupation and commenced reno-vating the property to create a family home alongside a small café. On one of their first nights in the house, Mr Bryant was awoken at three o'clock in the morning by the sound of shouting and laughter outside. Peering out of the window, he perceived four young children playing on the moor-land road in the moonlight. He watched them in bewilderment for several minutes before they suddenly vanished into thin air.

Whilst this was a relatively benign mani-festation, the occurrences grew increasingly more alarming as the years went by. The usual low-level poltergeist activity was fre-quently observed; the Bryants grew used to strange noises and unexplained odours, flickering lights and mysterious footsteps, especially when they were performing structural alterations. And it was not just the family who experienced these distur-bances; friends, visitors and even innocent passers-by all bore witness to inexplicable occurrences at Greenfield Lodge.

On one occasion, a friend house-sitting for the Bryants whilst they were on holiday was disturbed by the sensation of a woman's dress brushing past her as she reclined on a settee in the dining room. She looked up to see the kitchen door open and close of its

Greenfield Lodge, Scammonden.

own accord as a bitter chill crept into the air. Meanwhile, the lady who delivered the Bryants' milk experienced a similar phenomenon when she pulled up at the lodge early one morning. Suddenly, she grew convinced that she was not alone in the van and before she had a chance to get out herself, witnessed the passenger door open and shut, as if some invisible companion was disembarking.

In perhaps the most troubling and enigmatic incident, the Bryants were woken in the night by the screech of tyres on the tarmac outside. They looked out of their window to see a car pull up in the middle of the road, while its driver seemed to be examining the locked gate of a paddock directly opposite the lodge. A woman proceeded to get out of the passenger seat of the car and they heard her say, 'Let's get out of here – it came out of there,' pointing straight towards the house with a look of abject terror on her face.

The Bryants had three children and as they grew older, they also came into contact with whatever was troubling their home, especially on an upstairs landing which appeared to be the focus for the haunting. It was here that the youngest child, Andrew, saw an unfamiliar man dragging on a cigarette. The family had been plagued by the smell of tobacco smoke for many years, even though nobody in the house indulged, but before Andrew could approach and demand an explanation, the man leapt down the stairs and promptly disappeared.

The eldest child, Malcolm, had an even more unnerving encounter on the same landing. On his way to bed one evening, he was confronted by the figure of a woman wearing a long grey dress with her hair in a bun. She seemed upset, with her fingers clasped to her face as if she was crying. As Malcolm drew near, she removed her hands and to his horror, the boy saw that whilst the rest of the figure appeared substantial, there was nothing but mist where her face ought to be. She too vanished before his eyes.

When writer Terence Whitaker visited Greenfield Lodge in 1983 for his book *Yorkshire's Ghosts and Legends*, he determined from an inspection of the deeds that the female ghost was probably that of Elizabeth Emmett, who had died in the house in 1834. However, even this veteran investigator of the paranormal was troubled by the atmosphere of the place and concluded his passage on the haunting with an ominous note: 'I got the feeling that the house itself is not friendly towards prying strangers. Although it was a nice warm day, the house felt chilled and I was not sorry to turn my back on it.'

The Headless Horseman, Linthwaite

The village of Linthwaite was probably founded by Norse settlers prior to the Norman Conquest and for many centuries it remained a contained rural settlement, sparsely populated and largely isolated from the rest of the world. With the coming of the Industrial Revolution, textile mills proliferated in the district and as a result, the village now straggles the bottom of the Colne Valley between Milnsbridge and Slaithwaite, whilst high-density terraced housing sits cheek-by-jowl with the relics of an older epoch.

Constructed in the late sixteenth century, Linthwaite Hall would have been the nucleus of the original community and is perhaps best known today for its unique cruck-trussed barn which has been designated a Grade II listed building in recognition of its architectural significance. However, in days gone by, the vicinity was famed for quite a different reason and the persistence of that feeling well into the nineteenth century indicates it was not just the architecture of that more superstitious age which survived the Industrial Revolution in Linthwaite.

For generations, the locals lived in fear of glimpsing the headless horseman who was believed to career down the surrounding lanes at dusk. In 1859, the historian Charles Hobkirk even spoke to one man whose uncle had witnessed the spectre sometime in the early part of that century, watering his steed at a well near the hall. Hobkirk tells us that the villagers believed the horseman to be the spirit of 'some old chieftain, whom the neighbours call "a petty king"... and [who] for some misdemeanour against the Crown was beheaded in some fields nigh at hand.'

Whatever the true origin of the belief, it is notable that headless apparitions are a common trope in English tradition, although the reason why is unclear. Possibly because the head has long been perceived as the seat of the soul, it is entirely natural that a ghost should appear without it. Yet despite the ubiquity of headless ghosts, social historian Owen Davies notes, 'It is also the rarest of first-hand ghost sightings, based more on legend than experience,' making the recorded sighting of the Linthwaite horseman significant in the annals of folklore.

The headless motif also seems to have some curious resonance in this reach of the Colne Valley. In the neighbouring town of Slaithwaite, there is a public house called The Silent Woman, the sign of which

Above *Linthwaite Old Hall, Linthwaite.*
Right *The Silent Woman inn sign, Slaithwaite.*

proudly displays a headless lady in eighteenth-century garments. The inn opened
in 1782 and local legend claims that one of
the earliest landlords cut off his wife's head
in a murderous rage, whereupon her decap-
itated body ran outside just as a horse and
cart drove past. The animal is supposed to
have reared up and bolted at this gruesome
sight and since then, all horses have refused
to pass along that fateful stretch of road.

The Bull's Head, Blackmoorfoot

The Bull's Head is one of the focal points
of Blackmoorfoot, an old hamlet huddled
beneath the dam of a Victorian reservoir on
Crosland Moor. It was built in 1843 by John
and Sidney Lunn, brothers who had seemingly grown prosperous through the cattle
trade. However, the cellars of their public
house held the dark secret behind their
success. Beneath a trapdoor in the pathway
outside, the underground chambers were

The Bull's Head, Blackmoorfoot.

ular sightings of an unknown man wearing a flat cap, who would subsequently disappear. But the incident that cold February night was more than just rumour; it was a substantial manifestation in front of multiple witnesses.

Landlord David Dobson recalled that shortly before last orders, an incongruous-looking man entered the bar. He bought a drink, sat down in a corner and then left almost straight away. Unnerved by the stranger's odd countenance and behaviour, one of the regulars followed him to the door only to find that the man had vanished altogether. Mr Dobson told the local newspaper, 'He called us out and all we could see in the snow was a line of footprints from the pub door, down the side and ending at a blocked-up door. There were no more prints going away from it . . . No one could see how he left without making prints in the snow.'

Nobody was left in any doubt as to what had transpired and the landlord insisted, 'I know what we saw and it certainly was strange,' adding that the door at which the footsteps stopped had been boarded up for many years. Could the mystery visitor have been the ghost of John Lunn, retracing the steps he would have taken over a century and a half ago as he went to check on his ill-gotten merchandise, actions that ultimately resulted in his banishment to a strange and hostile country from which he could never escape in his lifetime?

stocked not with barrels of ale but piles of finest quality cloth, illicitly obtained and waiting to be sold on.

In those days, small manufacturers would hang their wares outside their workshops to dry, allowing the Lunns' lackeys to liberate choice pieces and surreptitiously dispose of them through the trapdoor outside the Bull's Head. The police force was barely established in the area at the time and the Lunns got away with their racket for a long while. Nonetheless, justice eventually caught up with the pair and they were sentenced to transportation to Botany Bay in Australia. Sidney served his time and made his way back to the Colne Valley many years later, but John died in the penal colony without ever seeing his home again.

Perhaps, however, he found a way to return after all. In 2010, staff and customers at the Bull's Head were puzzled by an inexplicable visitation one winter's night when snow lay thick on the ground all about. There had long been rumours about the pub. Employees often complained about the sound of footsteps overhead when they were locking up at night, despite being alone in the building, whilst there were reg-

The Standedge Tunnels

Burrowing deep beneath the bleak Pennine moors between Marsden and Saddleworth, the four Standedge tunnels are universally known as a remarkable testament to nineteenth-century enterprise. Over 3 miles long and more than 600 feet below the surface at their deepest point, they represent a significant achievement of enduring fascination to transport and engineering enthusiasts alike. Even today, the last working tunnel acts as an essential artery in the modern rail network, facilitating a fast link between the north-east and north-west of the country.

However, the Standedge tunnels have also gained a more sinister reputation. Subterranean concourses have long been a source of fear and fascination. Our pagan ancestors perceived caves and potholes as entrances to the Otherworld from whence unearthly powers might emerge, whilst belief concerning the spirit of the mines persisted well beyond the Industrial Revolution amongst those who worked them.

It is scarcely surprising that similar stories have attached themselves to these modern fissures into the very bowels of the earth. Moreover, with three of the tunnels closed for many years, an atmosphere of neglect and decay settled over Standedge, an atmosphere in which dark suspicions began to fester. Generations of Colne Valley children have peered through the grills fencing off the portals and wondered what secrets were hidden in those murky, forbidden depths.

A Watery Grave

The canal tunnel was the first of the tunnels to be bored at Standedge and it remains the longest example of its kind in Britain. Built between 1794 and 1811, the construction process was beset by difficulties. Nobody had counted on the sheer difficulty of keeping the workings free from water seeping through the gritstone above, whilst major floods devastated the project in both 1799

and 1808. Meanwhile, poor workmanship and inaccurate surveying caused numerous setbacks and it was only with the intervention of the renowned engineer Thomas Telford that the scheme was finished at all.

When the tunnel finally received its official opening on 4 April 1811, it had vastly exceeded its original cost projections and claimed the lives of over fifty navvies. Despite the extraordinary effort expended on the tunnel, its heyday lasted little more than thirty years before the railways rendered canal haulage obsolete. By the end of the nineteenth century, its fortunes were in terminal decline and the last commercial vessel passed the length of the tunnel on 6 November 1921. In 1944, an Act of Parliament decommissioned the Huddersfield Narrow Canal, seemingly closing the tunnel for good.

However, with the latter half of the twentieth century came an interest in industrial history and a recognition of the many leisure opportunities afforded by the country's neglected network of inland waterways. The Huddersfield Narrow Canal Society was founded in 1974 and began to work towards reopening the canal. Finally, a £5 million restoration project saw Standedge canal tunnel returned to its former glory and as of May 2001 it was once again fully navigable. Today, the Marsden portal at Tunnel End is the site of a major visitor centre, running numerous trips into the tunnel, whilst private vessels may pass through by appointment.

British Waterways, who are now responsible for the Huddersfield Narrow Canal, allegedly do not encourage fanciful tales about the tunnel. Despite the intrinsically dank and uncanny atmosphere of such a place, they market it as a family attraction and fear such stories might discourage children or those of a nervous disposition.

Standedge canal tunnel, Marsden. (Caitlin Sagan)

But whilst bluff bargeman Fred Carter told the *Yorkshire Post*, 'I have not seen any ghosts. I'm not frightened of this tunnel,' other employees have recorded strange experiences in its vicinity.

An anonymous female member of staff told the same newspaper, 'A few years ago some people claimed to have seen pink orbs – the residue of people who have died. One time there were a lot of noises in the tunnel that I have never heard before . . . Some people were frightened and walked out. They were really spooked.' Perhaps unusual acoustic effects are to be expected in a tunnel of Standedge's age and length, but when a place has a tragic history, such sounds unavoidably attain a darker significance.

Many commentators believe that fifty is a conservative reckoning for the number of workers who died during construction and possibly only represents an estimate for one end of the tunnel. Meanwhile, throughout its history, the Huddersfield Narrow Canal has been notorious for accidental drownings and suicides, Tunnel End in particular. A total of 250 deaths were recorded in its depths between 1917 and 1936 alone. Staring into the penumbral mouth of the tunnel on a gloomy day, it is easy to believe that the forlorn spirits of all those to have died in its embrace trouble the waters still.

However, perhaps the most instructive incident occurred during the tunnel's operational prime. As the builders had failed to provide a towpath inside the tunnel or devise any successful method of mechanical propulsion, throughout its working history barges were driven through Standedge by an arduous technique known as 'legging'. As one contemporary source explained,

'The men have to lie on their backs, and paw with their feet against the top or sides of the tunnel for three hours and upwards, till they have pushed the vessel through.' Such was the effort involved that from 1833 the Huddersfield Canal Company was obliged to provide its own dedicated teams of leggers to increase efficiency.

In late 1836, just such a team was working a barge through the tunnel when one of their number suddenly released 'an apparently causeless, piercing scream', and in his panic stumbled into the inky waters never to be seen alive again. The canal company was subsequently forced to drain the tunnel in order to recover his corpse but during their search they made a far grimmer discovery. Not far from where they ultimately found the body of the unfortunate boatman, the decaying cadaver of a young woman was revealed. It was clear that before being flung into the water, her throat had been savagely cut.

The question of what had happened to the girl was never resolved, nor the mystery of exactly what the legger had witnessed to cause him such distress. Had he seen her lifeless eyes gazing back at him from beneath the surface of the water? It seems unlikely that in the tenebrous conditions of the tunnel, anybody could have discerned such a sight. Had he perhaps, therefore, been confronted with a vision of the girl's tormented wraith, desperately trying to lead people to her mortal remains and so secure some measure of justice?

This may have been the opinion of Tom Rolt, founder of the Inland Waterways Association (IWA) and one of the very few to have navigated Standedge canal tunnel during its many years of closure. In 1948, he traversed its depths in a leaking barge, alongside co-founder of the IWA, Robert Aickman, and Aickman's then-paramour,

Elizabeth Jane Howard. Curiously, all three present on the expedition went on to become acclaimed writers of supernatural fiction and in the same year as his trip through Standedge, Rolt published a ghost story titled 'Bosworth Summit Pound'. Significantly, the tale concerns a canal tunnel haunted by the ghost of a murdered girl whose corpse had been cast into one of the ventilation shafts of the tunnel.

Spirit Tracks

The first railway tunnel beneath Standedge was completed in 1849, accommodating a single-gauge track to the south of the canal tunnel and at a slightly higher level. As traffic increased, a second single-gauge tunnel was bored and opened in 1871. Even this was insufficient to meet demand, however, forcing the construction of a third railway tunnel by 1894, this time large enough to admit a double-gauge track. The single-gauge tunnels continued to carry freight until they were closed in 1963 as part of Dr Beeching's programme of rail cuts, whereupon they became the focus of more ominous pursuits.

The tunnels certainly have a unique atmosphere. In certain conditions, the differential between the exterior and interior temperature, along with the proximity to the canal, causes a thick mist to build. Meanwhile, there are frequent disconcerting gusts of wind and changes in air pressure caused by trains running through the adjacent 1891 tunnel. Such places have always held fascination for self-styled 'urban explorers', not to mention less historically-minded trespassers, but in the early 1980s anybody venturing into the tunnels was confronted by terrifying evidence to suggest they were not the only ones to have entered those forbidden depths.

The two single-gauge tunnels are linked in the middle by a vaulted cross-heading nicknamed 'The Cathedral' and it was here that several sources reported disturbing the remains of occult ritual activity. Initially, workmen maintaining the tunnels stumbled upon cabbalistic sigils inscribed on the walls and a magic circle painted on the ground, in which two sheep skulls had been placed. Yet despite the workmen reporting their discovery to the police, it seems that whoever had placed them there was not deterred.

Years later, a one-time trespasser recalled finding further signs of esoteric ceremonies:

> A large painted image of the sun with a demonic face, and on the other side that of the moon, again with sinister features . . . On the flagstone floor was a large double circle; within it occult symbols were etched and burnt-out candles lay in wax pools around the perimeter of the circle. In one corner of this central room lay the headless carcass of a cockerel, still stained with blood. I will never forget the dark feeling that came over me.

One group of adventurers had an even closer encounter. Despite being warned by some local children not to proceed as they had seen robed men entering the tunnel, and later the light of a fire flickering beyond, the group set off through the Marsden portal. Their journey to Diggle was uneventful but on their return, they were plunged into a shocking confrontation with a shrieking figure, whose visage seemed to be concealed behind some grotesque mask. It ran flailing towards them, striking one of the party as it passed, before vanishing into shadow. Who knows what entities were invoked in the bowels of Standedge by its resident coven and left to stalk the warrens for evermore?

Access remains popular with urban explorers today and a recent entrant described another odd experience:

> One phenomenon we couldn't explain was the strange flickering light we saw about 2 miles into the tunnel. At first we thought it was daylight at the far end. That was until it started swaying from side to side. We watched it for a bit before deciding it was coming towards us. It must have been a strange effect created by the air pressure . . . or . . . well we never saw the ghostly spectre of an old railway man coming our way with a swinging lamp thankfully!

Even the last working train tunnel is not free from supernatural disturbance. A former railway man who worked on the line before privatisation recalled how the period 10.05 to 10.15 p.m. was so ill-omened that eventually British Rail was forced to ensure that nothing entered the tunnel during this period. Supposedly all electrics tended to malfunction and even gas lamps would fail, plunging everything into darkness. More alarmingly still, trains would mysteriously slow down, leaving their engineers to struggle with the controls and a gnawing conviction that some terrible event would befall them should they allow the vehicle to grind to a halt.

The Marsden Moors

Rising to some 1,500 feet above sea level, the high moorland enclosing the upper reaches of the Colne Valley is widely reckoned to be some of the most desolate territory in England. Vast tracts of peat bog – always ready to swallow the unwary traveller – seem to paint the landscape black, whilst misshapen gritstone excrescences loom on every horizon, clawing at the louring sky. Weather conditions can change rapidly here; as clouds congeal around the tops, anybody unfortunate enough to be crossing that terrain can suddenly find themselves stumbling blindly into the fog, defenceless as the surrounding country is scoured by wind and rain.

It is scarcely any wonder that our ancestors personified the elemental forces that govern these summits, and the hills hereabouts were long known as the haunt of fearsome beings such as boggarts and barguests. Over the ridge in Saddleworth, 'boggarts took the form of a large round woolsack with red eyes as big as dinner plates,' whilst a stretch of hillside called Holme, above Slaithwaite, was well known as 'a rendezvous for ghosts . . . [where] crying boggarts were plentiful'. But whilst tales of boggarts died out generations ago, perhaps the phenomena that inspired them did not.

The Phantom Horsemen of Buckstones

The A640 across Buckstones Moss, also known as New Hey Road, is a lonely highway indeed. Between the colourfully-named Nont Sarah's Hotel at Scammonden and the Saddleworth village of Denshaw, there is not a single inhabited dwelling for at least 6 miles. The only building to break the isolation is the derelict shell of Buckstones House, a notorious den of thieves in centuries past. In 1903, this remote area was also the scene of a brutal double murder, when two gamekeepers were shot dead and the bodies left to rot amongst the bog-cotton and heather. Their killer was never brought to justice.

It was on this road in 1968 that policeman Phil Clay had a strange encounter which haunted him for decades afterwards. Clay was a constable attached to the Road Traffic Division and stationed in the Saddleworth village of Uppermill, which in those days was still part of Yorkshire's West Riding. One clear but blustery autumn night, Clay was returning to Uppermill following a visit to the divisional headquarters in Huddersfield. He had chosen to travel the longer but more scenic route of the A640 and to take full advantage of the seclusion, he had cut his headlights, opting instead for his sidelights and the illumination of a full moon.

A little over a mile beyond Nont Sarah's Hotel, Clay saw three horsemen emerge from the darkness ahead. As a policeman, his first thought was to stop and reprimand them for their lack of stirrup lights, but as he drew closer he realised there was something unusual about their appearance. Two of the riders were dressed in the style of seventeenth-century gentry, resplendent in their bicorne hats, velvet coats and deerskin breaches. The third appeared to be a peasant of the same era, wearing a homespun shirt, leather doublet and neckerchief, leading a packhorse behind them. Clay also noticed that the two gentlemen carried swords and pistols.

The somewhat puzzled policeman slowed down as he passed the party but as they failed to acknowledge him, he turned round and drove alongside again. Still they seemed unaware of his presence. He then attempted a third pass, fully intending to stop his car and inquire as to their reasons for being out so oddly-attired in the middle of nowhere late at night. However, it was not to be. Clay later recalled:

> As I slowly approached, the leading horseman acknowledged me by bowing

61

The lonely A640 across Buckstones, Marsden.

Redbrook Clough, Marsden. (Caitlin Sagan)

as he touched his right hand to the brim of his hat. At this point a cold shiver ran down my spine and I decided that discretion was the better part of valour . . . so I pushed my foot down on the accelerator and made a rapid departure towards civilisation, home and safety.

Although he never told his colleagues in the force at the time for fear of ribbing, Clay remained troubled by his experience and so, masquerading as an anonymous motorist, contacted the newsdesk of the *Huddersfield Daily Examiner*. He reported the sighting and inquired if there had been any charity rides or fancy-dress parties in that area which might account for it, but a journalist later got in touch to say they had been unable to find any record of such activity on the night in question. Clay never got any closer to an explanation and many years later, the memory of that mysterious incident vexes the retired policeman still.

The Ghost That Never Was

As if the treacherous terrain was not enough, brigandry was rife on the Marsden moors during previous centuries and the toponymy of the area still testifies to its impact on the local psyche. Thieves Clough descends from Standedge towards the Great Western Hotel, forming a tributary of the deeper Redbrook Clough, whose upper reaches are now submerged by one of the reservoirs built to feed the Huddersfield Narrow Canal, snaking through the rock several hundred feet below.

Prior to construction of the reservoir, the head of Redbrook Clough was the site of a toll bar on the old Manchester road and at this time, traders from the Colne Valley would regularly pass by in the early hours of the morning to reach the city markets before dawn. However, waggoners rarely liked to travel that route alone. Not only were there rumours that the gatekeeper was in cahoots with highwaymen and footpads, still darker talk circulated about the Boggart of Redbrook Clough who accosted merchants on their way to market, causing such fright that they often upped sticks and fled, abandoning their wares in that lonely spot.

Then one night, a bold waggoner by the name of Rodgers glimpsed the apparition readying to beset him. Rather than turning heel, Rodgers stood his ground and, as one contemporary writer put it, 'commenced to exorcise the ghost in a novel manner, by blows from a heavy whipstock'. In fact, the 'boggart' turned out to be one of the infamous footpads in disguise and Rodgers proceeded to tie the villain to his wagon and parade him around the nearby inns, thereby ensuring that all his fellow travellers saw the sham exposed.

But whilst this manifestation of the Boggart of Redbrook Clough may have been nothing more than a robber's ruse, the fact that it was so effective clearly demonstrates the hold such stories once had over the local imagination. It may even be that stories of a boggart at Redbrook circulated long before the felons thought to turn them to their advantage. The surrounding moors have their fair share of 'Boggart Stones', and as the gales howl through these malformed outcrops and the mist seethes, it is possible to believe that ancient terrors still slumber in such places, just waiting to be disturbed.

5

The Parishes of Kirkburton and Emley

Lane Head House, Shepley

The oldest part of Lane Head House was constructed in the late sixteenth century and for many generations it was home to the Firth family, who became one of the first prominent Quaker dynasties in the region. Permission for a Meeting House was officially given in 1696; originally this was a temporary structure, but it was incorporated into the main building in 1709, making it contemporary with the more famous (and still used) Friends' Meeting House at High Flatts nearby.

Supernatural disturbances were successively reported at Lane Head House throughout the nineteenth century. The Firth family were once bothered by 'curious tappings and hammerings and ringings in the night', which they initially believed to be tailors working late in one of the neighbouring outbuildings in preparation for Shepley Fest. One night, the cacophony became so persistent and infuriating that the patriarch of the family decided to investigate and ask whoever it was to keep the noise down. Yet a thorough search revealed no culprit and still the sound continued, leaving the family so afraid that all six slept together in a single room that night.

A later occupant was alone in the house one night on St Valentine's Day, caring for her sick infant, and, as midnight drew near, she decided to retire. Ascending the stairs with the child clutched in her arms, she was shocked to confront the hazy figure of a woman on the landing. The mother closed her eyes and ignored the apparition as she continued towards her room. Just as she closed the door, she took a glimpse back along the passage and saw the phantom fully. The ghost was that of an old, plainly dressed woman with long silver hair parted in the middle. Tears were rolling down her cheeks as she stared back, 'sadly and sternly'.

The mother resolved to keep the experience to herself, knowing that her husband would just dismiss her fears, whilst she did not want to alarm the superstitious household staff. However, a little while later one of the maids returned from an errand in Shepley village with a local tale that every year at midnight on St Valentine's Day, the house was haunted by the ghost of an elderly Quaker lady, who wandered the corridors in a state of distress as she attempted to find a hidden treasure. Another version claimed the woman met an untimely end in the house on that date.

Lane Head House, Shepley.

Phantom ladies are one of the most common apparitions in English ghost lore, and it is not surprising to find one associated with a building of this vintage. It is also a common motif for such revenants to be guarding or searching for lost treasure in a state of distress. The explanation given for the spirit's presence at Lane Head House, however, seems suspect. St Valentine's Day held no significance for the Quakers and they were not known for owning 'treasure' – indeed, their women often spurned any form of personal decoration. It may, therefore, have been an apocryphal narrative that borrows a number of related tropes, designed to explain an existent haunting.

The Sovereign Inn, Shepley

A familiar sight to travellers on the A629 between Huddersfield and Sheffield, the Sovereign Inn is one of the most famous hostelries in the district and numerous traditions have grown up around it. The name of the establishment is the subject of a romantic narrative, which claims that around 1829, its founder, Seth Senior, was an itinerant tinsmith, who called at Lane Head House one cold winter's night, explaining that his wife had gone into labour in an adjacent field and begging for assistance.

The Firth family, who owned Lane Head House at the time, not only came to the

The Sovereign Inn, Shepley.

Seniors' aid, they took the family in over the winter months, employing them as servants and accommodating them over the coach house. When spring came, Mr Firth presented Seth with a gold sovereign for his labours. The tinsmith used this to rent a nearby cottage, where he began to brew beer from local spring water. This was the birth of the Sovereign Inn, an enterprise that flourished until the Senior family owned several pubs and breweries in the Shepley area.

Two ghosts are reputed to haunt the Sovereign Inn. The first is that of Elizabeth Smith, a fondly remembered landlady there during the early twentieth century. Her perfume has been smelt mysteriously wafting through the pub, whilst the apparition of a lady has been seen at one of the upper windows. The second spectre is of a more tragic nature. In 1965, a particularly inebriated customer mistook the cellar door for the exit and tumbled down the stairs, breaking his neck in the process. Bar staff have since encountered his unhappy spirit roaming those subterranean depths and many animals refuse to enter at all.

Curiously, the Seniors' original cottage, which is attached to the present inn, used to display a crude stone carving of a head on one of its gables. Some have suggested that this was a depiction of Seth Senior himself, but its simple, stylised features indicated that it is was not meant to be a portrait of any single individual, but a representation of the head 'archetype'. Such carvings are typically known as 'archaic stone heads' and were a mode of folk art which flourished in the South Pennines between the sixteenth and nineteenth century. Some have even claimed that this tradition showed an unbroken line of descent from prehistoric cultures in the region.

Typically, the purpose of such carvings was not for decoration, but to ward off evil. They were typically placed at 'liminal' locations – thresholds and boundaries such as doorways, windows, gables or chimneys – through which the pre-modern, superstitious mind believed malign supernatural forces could gain access to the building. As late as 1971, the landlord of the Old Sun Inn at Haworth placed a carved head above the doorway in order to lay a ghost that was troubling the premises to rest. The example at the Sovereign Inn has disappeared in recent years and perhaps this explains why it is so troubled by ghosts.

Another story suggests that the archaic stone head at the Sovereign Inn was carved to commemorate a worker who had met an accidental death during construction of the building. This motif is attached to many such carvings and some folklorists have argued that it indicates the head served as a substitute for 'foundation sacrifice'. This tradition was practiced by many prehistoric societies in the British Isles to ensure good fortune for a new building, and required the body of a sacrifice to be placed in the foundations of the structure. Typically, an animal was used but, in some cases, human remains have been found in this context.

Carr Lane, Shepley

Now an inconspicuous backwater, at one point the hamlet of Shepley Carr was a principle settlement along the packhorse road between Huddersfield and Penistone. The small huddle of dwellings is dominated by Carr House, which in the early nineteenth century was the residence of the Tinker family, a lineage primarily remembered in the district for the construction of the Tinker Monument, a folly whose ruins can still be seen on the hills above the Holme Valley.

It seems that one of the Tinker patriarchs was a 'wild, hectoring type of individual'. By all accounts, this character was obsessed with hunting and would ride the hills all day with his hounds – often carelessly across his neighbours' land – before returning to the homestead to drink and carouse the night away. Suffice it to say, he was not popular in the district and few were sorry when he died at quite a considerable age.

However, it transpired that Tinker was not going to permit death to prevent him from terrorising his neighbours. One night, following his passing, an elderly subsequent resident of Carr House was disturbed by a blood-curdling howl, causing her hair to prick up like 'nine pins on a door mat'. Presently, she heard the sound of the horses

Carr Lane, Shepley.

whinnying and kicking in the stables, but whilst she attempted to ignore the cacophony, it persisted until she realised she would have to venture out into the darkness to investigate.

The old woman found the stables locked as she had left them, but as she unfastened the doors and thrust her candle inside, she was confronted by the horses stamping and frothing at the mouth in fright. The animals bolted and as the woman fled, she caught a fearful glimpse of the source of their terror. It was the pallid spectre of Tinker, risen from the grave to indulge in a final hunt. Indeed, some locals say that his ghost can be seen riding down Carr Lane on stormy nights still.

The Old Tannery, Thurstonland

Prior to the scientific advances of the last two centuries, the process by which animal skins were tanned to create leather represented one of the most unpleasant jobs in human history. It involved immersing the hides in vats of human urine or animal faeces, and such was the noisome reputation of the industry that tanneries were typically sited on the periphery of a settlement, downwind of the principle residential areas. As the Industrial Revolution progressed, improved methods of tanning were devised and like so many other trades, it grew increasingly mechanised, rendering old tanneries obsolete.

Such was the case in the picturesque village of Thurstonland, which occupies an elevated hilltop location above the Holme Valley, and in the early twentieth century was known for the longest life-expectancy in England. The tannery had been one of the biggest employers in the village since the eighteenth century but following the transformation of the industry, it closed in 1910. The building was subsequently used as a barn until 1960, when it was converted into a distinguished dwelling house. The old tan pit was covered over, but occupants of the house have been disturbed by more than the lingering odour of the site's former use.

In the evenings, unaccountable footsteps have been heard on the gravel around the old tan pit outside. Then, in the middle of the night, the sound of feet can again be heard, now on the external stairs. The steps proceed through a locked door and across the floor, accompanied by the noise of a chair dragged along in their wake. The first owner of the house refused to believe his wife and daughter when they told him of their experiences, but he was forced to revise his opinion when a loaf of bread launched itself across the room and struck him on the head. Thereafter, he kept open Bibles in every room to discourage further visitants.

When the residents of the old tannery investigated possible reasons for the haunting, they were told of a tradition that sometime during the eighteenth century, one of the employees returned from a liquid lunch at one of the village hostelries,

The Old Tannery, Thurstonland.

fell into the tan pit and drowned in the festering waste – scarcely an easy death. It is now believed to be his troubled spirit that disturbs the peace of the tannery, especially as the disturbances are always most noticeable around the 23rd and 24th of the month, possibly the date on which the unfortunate tanner died.

The Old Corn Mill, Thunderbridge

Thunderbridge is a delightful, historic hamlet situated at a crossing of a stream known as the Thunder Bridge Dike as it flows towards Fenay Beck. Despite the proximity of the busy Penistone Road, the dense surrounding woodland and ancient buildings give the settlement an atmosphere of idyllic rural seclusion, which has led to it being designated a conservation area.

At one time, however, Thunderbridge would have been a bustling community, as the stream provided power for the district's principle corn mill, which stands a short distance from the eponymous bridge. Built at least 300 years ago, the mill continued to operate well into the twentieth century – one of the last traditional corn mills in the area – although it has now been converted into a private residence.

Around 1870, a man was crushed to death by machinery at the old corn mill and for a long while afterwards, local folk believed his ghost haunted the environs. The most notable sighting came from the sister of one Mrs G. A. Wood, who, as a young girl, had been playing on Grange Lane around twilight when she saw the figure of a man emerge from the corn mill and walk slowly up the road towards her.

At first she thought the figure was her father, but gradually she realised that whilst

The former corn mill, Thunderbridge.

there was an uncanny resemblance, this man was 'unlike him in some respects'. As the form drew closer, the sight of him seized the girl with a shivering fear and she ran home at full speed, only to find her father firmly ensconced within, eating his supper. The girl was so unnerved by her experience that she fell into a faint and was bedridden for several weeks afterwards.

Subsequent enquiries by her family revealed that no local had been abroad in the vicinity of the corn mill that evening and from the description of the man given by the girl, most residents of the hamlet agreed that she had seen the ghost of the tragically killed miller. Perhaps most significantly, the unfortunate victim had been a cousin of the girl's father and they had closely resembled each other in both countenance and stature.

Storthes Hall, Kirkburton

Although the Storthes family gave their name to this area of wooded countryside between Kirkburton and Farnley Tyas in the Middle Ages – whilst their successors, the Horsfalls, built a handsome mansion there in the late eighteenth century – it is not as an ancestral seat that the name of Storthes Hall is primarily known. To many long-standing residents of the Huddersfield district, it will forever be associated with the sprawling psychiatric hospital that operated on the site from 1904 until 1991. Indeed, in the local vernacular, Storthes Hall was long a synonym for Bedlam.

With forty-six wards and around 2,000 patients, Storthes Hall Mental Hospital (as it was originally known) was one of the largest establishments of its type in the country.

Within the medical establishment, it was generally regarded as a progressive institution. However, in its early days – before mental illness was properly understood – it was doubtless the scene of much cruelty and degradation. Until 1969, wards were strictly segregated by sex (including the staff) and family members were discouraged from having contact with the patients.

As the twentieth century wore on, new medical treatments for mental illness, alongside government schemes such as care in the community, reduced the need for psychiatric hospitals of Storthes Hall's capacity and it closed in 1991. The majority of the complex was raised to the ground and the land was redeveloped as the site of Huddersfield University's student accommodation. Only a few buildings remain from the old hospital; one former ward has been converted into a bar, whilst both the former mortuary and administration block still stand derelict with an uncertain future.

Since the demolition of the hospital, Storthes Hall's fearful reputation has not been especially diminished. The atmosphere of the area has variously been described as 'wrong' and 'tainted', whilst one witness claims to have been overwhelmed by 'gibbering horror' in the vicinity. For some years, the former hospital mortuary was used by the university drama department to store equipment. Many students, and even university staff, would not enter the building alone due to the feeling of dread and sickness that seized many people within.

Numerous supernatural reports have also emerged from the newly-built student accommodation. Posters have been found ripped from the walls of locked rooms overnight; showers have turned themselves on without any human agency; the unaccountable sound of scratching or banging is regularly heard from around the doors and ceilings. Some individuals have even reported waking in the middle of the night, only to see indistinct figures skulking in the shadows of their room.

Perhaps such phenomena can be put down to hysterical imaginings, invoked by a corpus of folk motifs that already associate former asylums with supernatural activity. Such abandoned hospitals have become well known in the United States for an activity folklorists have dubbed 'legend-tripping', which sees groups of

Former ward block at Storthes Hall, Kirkburton.

Huddersfield University student accommodation at Storthes Hall, Kirkburton.

Derelict administration building at Storthes Hall, Kirkburton.

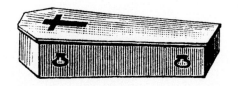

people – usually adolescents – venture into 'spooky' places at night in order to confront some vaguely defined supernatural threat. The pursuit is typically analysed as a rite of passage or communal bonding exercise and whilst 'legend-tripping' has been less well studied in the UK, it is undoubtedly widespread.

The surviving buildings at Storthes Hall amply fulfil the legend-trip criteria and the dilapidated administration block in particular has become a favoured nocturnal destination for intrepid students – not to mention urban explorers and paranormal investigators, who are essentially performing a similar ritual. A number of unofficial paranormal investigations have been conducted in the crumbling edifice; one group claims to have witnessed the figure of man disappearing through a closed door and heard mysterious screams wrack the building.

Discussion of the supernatural activity at Storthes Hall has tended to focus on the former psychiatric hospital as the source of the phenomena. Some believe it to be a psychic imprint of the distress and trauma that must once have been highly concentrated in that place, whilst others bandy apocryphal stories of grisly suicides and nurses murdered by disturbed patients. However, it is a curious fact that the environs of Storthes Hall were thought to be haunted many years before the hospital came to occupy the site.

The historian Philip Ahier records a tradition that during the nineteenth century, the woodland around Storthes Hall was widely feared by the local populace. Many years before, a resident of the district had buried his wife in those woods, as she had loved them so dearly during her lifetime – a story subsequently confirmed when a party of gamekeepers out rabbiting accidentally stumbled across her coffin. As the lady had not been buried in consecrated ground, tales that her unquiet spirit stalked the trees were rife in the neighbourhood and many people avoided the area on that account.

It is possible that some objective phenomenon produces anomalous experiences around Storthes Hall, which are then interpreted according to the prevailing folkloric paradigm. In the highly religious nineteenth century, unconsecrated burial was a source of superstitious fear and ghosts were always regarded as the spirits of the dead. Conversely, in the largely secular twenty-first century, mental illness is still widely regarded with dread, whilst believers frequently regard the supernatural as a sort of psychic residue. It seems that whatever the truth behind the experiences at Storthes Hall, they have undoubtedly been filtered through the lens of their day.

The Old Vicarage, Kirkburton

A Grade I listed building, All Hallows' Church at Kirkburton is one of the most ancient in the Huddersfield area, its earliest features dating from 1190. The Old Vicarage, which stands behind high walls just across the road from the church, is also of a rare vintage, constructed in the early seventeenth century. It is a substantial building and due to the ever-rising cost of heating and maintenance, the Church was forced to sell this asset in 1985. The minister now resides in a considerably more modest house nearby, whilst the Old Vicarage itself has been converted into a private dwelling.

The Old Vicarage, Kirkburton.

During that period of strife known as the English Civil Wars, the incumbent at All Hallows' was one Reverend Gamaliel Whitaker, who lived at the Old Vicarage with his wife, Hester. Reverend Whitaker was a notorious Royalist sympathiser, which made him unpopular amongst many members of his congregation, who primarily supported the Parliamentarian cause. He was ousted from his position in March 1642, although, if the following story has any truth in it, he must have gone on living at the vicarage.

In early 1643, a troop of Royalist soldiers under the command of the Earl of Newcastle attacked Holmfirth. It seems that local sentiment blamed Reverend Whitaker for instigating this outrage, for on the night of 12 January, a contingent of Parliamentarians proceeded to Kirkburton to arrest the turbulent priest. In the ensuing skirmish, Hester Whitaker was hit by a stray bullet and died on the staircase of the vicarage. Distraught at this tragedy, her husband surrendered and was carried away to prison in Manchester, where he died little over a fortnight later from 'grief and ill-usage'.

Whilst the English Civil Wars produced many apocryphal traditions, it seems that there is some substance in the tale of Hester Whitaker's demise. The Kirkburton parish registers record that she was 'slain' on 12 January 1643 and buried three days later, whilst an inscribed epitaph to Reverend

Gamaliel Whitaker was once to be seen at Manchester Cathedral, giving the date of his death as 1 February 1643. It has also been reported that during renovation work at the vicarage in 1954, bones were discovered, which forensic examination revealed to be those of a woman – although if Hester was officially interred after her death, the connection is dubious.

The unfortunate end of Hester Whitaker lived on in the folk memory of Kirkburton for many centuries after the event. It was said that the bloodstain she left on the vicarage staircase could never be washed out (a popular motif connected with violent death) and, of course, that her restless spirit walked the building still. Perhaps owing to the nature of her demise – as an innocent victim in a primarily male conflict – her ghost was only supposed to appear to women. In the 1940s, the vicar's wife was profoundly disturbed by a presence walking around the room and brushing past her, although her husband experienced nothing.

Never let it be said, however, that the Church unburdened itself of the vicarage in order to escape the ghost. The last ecclesiastic to occupy the building scorned any such loose talk. Prior to the sale of the vicarage in 1985, when asked about the haunting by a local newspaper, the incumbent vicar answered pointedly, 'I attach no significance to it at all and in the two years we have lived here, we have had no experiences of any ghost.' Perhaps as the building's religious associations were severed, and

with them the last philosophical vestiges of the conflict in which she was killed, Hester Whitaker could rest more easily in her grave.

Emley Moor Colliery

Although the area is now most famous for its landmark transmitter mast (still the tallest freestanding structure in the United Kingdom), Emley Moor has a history of mining operations stretching back to the Middle Ages. Emley Moor Colliery itself first opened in the nineteenth century and by the 1980s, it was not only the westernmost pit in Yorkshire, but also the last to be still worked by hand. Like so many others, Emley Moor Colliery closed at the end of 1985 following the unsuccessful outcome of the previous year's Miners' Strike. Today, all the shafts are capped and a business park occupies the site.

Even in its later days, mining was an industry rife with superstition and Emley Moor Colliery was no different in this respect. Liz Linahan, who collected a number of stories from the South Yorkshire Coalfield, relates that one particular tunnel at Emley Moor was regarded with dread by the miners. One of the original workings, it had been bored beneath an old burial ground and unpleasant 'drippings' often seeped through the roof. Nobody cared to enter that tunnel alone: several miners claimed to have seen a phantom light swaying in the darkness down there, whilst another fled the pit in terror after glimpsing 'something indescribably horrible'.

Another report circulates, documenting the experience of a security guard following the closure of the colliery. Although the pit ceased operations on 20 December 1985, efforts to decommission and secure the workings continued for many months into 1986, during which time a security guard remained on site overnight. By this point, the electricity had been disconnected, leaving the guards with only a gas lamp for illumination and, owing to the unsafe nature of the buildings, they were not encouraged to patrol.

Nonetheless, one night the security guard on duty allowed boredom and curiosity to get the better of him and he embarked upon an exploration of the abandoned colliery. At a certain point, his light failed him, forcing him to negotiate his way back to the cabin in the all-enveloping darkness. As he stumbled on through the pitch black, he was surprised by a figure looming out of the darkness on the periphery of his vision. The figure hailed him and knowing that no other person was authorised to be on site, the guard deviated from his course to ascertain the trespasser's business and to forcibly evict him if necessary.

The intruder explained that he had once also worked as a nightwatchman at the pit and had come to take one last look around his old workplace before it was demolished altogether. Grateful for the company, the security guard took his predecessor back to the cabin for a cup of tea and they chatted for a long while about the colliery in its glory days. At some point during the early hours, the security guard dozed off and when he awoke, the erstwhile nightwatchman had taken his leave.

The following morning, the guard reported the incident to the National Coal Board officials supervising the decommissioning process, many of whom had worked at the colliery prior to its closure. They reacted with incredulity, claiming the description of the intruder exactly fitted that of a former nightwatchman who had been killed in an accident at the pit many years before. The security guard then took them to the place where he had encountered the apparition and realised, to his horror, that if the wraith had not diverted him from his original path, he would have plunged down an uncapped shaft to a certain death.

The Old Vicarage, Emley

Dating in part from the medieval period, the Church of St Michael the Archangel at Emley is another of the Huddersfield area's most venerable places of worship. A local legend suggests its location was chosen by the faeries, who thwarted the builders' attempts to construct the church at a different site by repeatedly moving the stones to the present spot by night. This narrative is commonly encountered in connection with ancient churches and a similar story is told of the Church of St John the Baptist at Kirkheaton.

The old church was once accompanied by an equally distinguished vicarage across the street. It was a substantial building, originally erected in the early seventeenth century and substantially enlarged in the Georgian period, with a stable block and extensive gardens. One source referred to it as 'perhaps the finest parsonage in the diocese'. Sadly, it became a financial burden and the Church sold the building in the 1950s. The Old Vicarage passed through a succession of private hands until it was finally demolished in 1969, allowing new houses to be built on the site. Today, only a street name – Rectory Lane – remains to testify to the vicarage's former location.

The last clergyman to occupy the vicarage was Reverend H.N. Pobjoy and, in 1952, his family reported experiencing a number of supernatural disturbances during their residency. This activity invariably manifested as the sound of the bulky front door being opened and shut – even when it was visibly shut and known to be locked – followed by a series of heavy footsteps along the hallway, which finally seemed to come to a halt at the door to the old kitchen cellar.

The phenomena occurred most often in the mornings and searches of the house revealed that nobody had entered on any of these instances. Yet, Reverend Pobjoy noted, 'The footsteps we occasionally hear are anything but ghost-like noises. The sound is loud and clear.' He also insisted, 'We are very happy here and the sounds do not disturb us. This is a very friendly old house and we arc certainly not anxious to have any further investigation made.' However, the inexplicable noises so unnerved his younger daughter that on one occasion, she barricaded herself in her room until they had ceased.

When the family made enquiries about the phenomena, the wife of a previous incumbent, Reverend Hayward, who had lived at the vicarage between 1901 and 1936, also claimed to have been troubled by the sound. She reported that the footsteps would continue through the old kitchen cellar door, down a flight of steps and across the room to the hearth, from where she would then hear the clattering of fire irons. The vicarage cellars were quite extensive – described as 'dark, winding subterranean passages' in one report – but by the Pobjoys' tenure, they had been shut up for many years.

One source indicated the disturbances might have been the restless spirit of a former vicar of the parish, who died on the premises following a fall from his horse. However, a more convincing suggestion was that the sounds were the lingering impression of a raid by Parliamentarian forces during the English Civil Wars. In 1643, Roundheads had supposedly searched the vicarage for the church silver, which had been removed from St Michael's and hidden in the vicarage cellars.

The George & Dragon, Flockton

A former mining community, the village of Flockton straggles along the side of the busy A637. The ever-increasing volume of traffic passing through the settlement has been a source of controversy in recent decades, but Flockton has always been associated with the highway, as the presence of venerable coaching inn, the George & Dragon attests. A distinctive, timber-frame building, it was constructed in the early sixteenth century and has provided a favoured sojourn for travellers ever since.

The George & Dragon was once known locally as the Chained Poker, owing to two remarkable fire irons that once hung in the main bar. In modern times, however, a resident ghost has supplied the pub with a new

The George & Dragon, Flockton.

talking point. Given the age of the structure and the amount of history its walls must have seen, this is scarcely surprising, although the nature of the spirit is vaguely defined.

Veteran researcher of the paranormal in West Yorkshire, Andy Owens records that during the 1970s the landlord and his wife were profoundly disturbed when at about half past three in the afternoon, the door to their private lounge seemed to open and close of its own accord. Despite a blazing fire, an icy chill descended over the room and lingered until the door did the same thing again, as if whatever entered had now left. The landlord was sufficiently concerned to search the pub, but no corporeal intruder was discovered.

Meanwhile, the figure of a man in eighteenth-century attire has been seen around the pub on several occasions, on the upstairs landing and in a disused room adjacent to the bar. A customer also saw two figures repeatedly pass the open door of the pub, but when he told the landlord, who

went to investigate, they had disappeared. The customer was so unnerved by the experience that he requested the landlord accompany him to his car when he left.

Such mysterious mirages seem to be a common phenomenon in Flockton. Owens also refers to the experience of an anonymous police officer patrolling the village at night, who once saw a group of strange figures prowl past him in the small hours. Thinking they might be a gang of burglars looking for likely pickings, the constable resolved to keep his eye on them. However, as soon as he tried to spot them again, they had vanished into thin air, despite there being nowhere to go.

The Old Vicarage, Flockton

Like the old rectories of nearby Emley and Kirkburton, the Church was forced to sell its substantial parsonage in Flockton to private individuals several decades ago. However,

The Old Vicarage, Flockton.

the similarities do not end there. The vicarage was similarly believed to be haunted, with rumour of the manifestations particularly prevalent in the mid-twentieth century, and whilst Flockton's narrative is scarcely as developed as its neighbours, you might start to wonder if haunted vicarages were once a conscious fashion in this part of the world.

The visitations primarily took the form of the sound of a bell ringing at unsociable hours and the rustling of an invisible skirt in the corridor. In 1958, Reverend Enoch Davies reported actually seeing an apparition on several occasions, although he does not actually describe it: 'The last time I came into contact with it was a few months ago. I was washing the breakfast things when it appeared . . . I have not seen it since.'

The family of the previous incumbent, Reverend M. Banister, had allegedly experienced a great deal of trouble from the ghost. The vicar was forced to conduct a blessing ceremony in the building in an attempt to exorcise the presence, although nobody seemed entirely sure to whom the spirit belonged; some whispered that a woman had been murdered in the building centuries previously, but that is a common trope and may be apocryphal.

Reverend Banister's efforts to expel the unwanted presence were unsuccessful and, still troubled by the disturbances, Reverend Davies requested heavier guns. He invited the new Bishop of Wakefield, the Right Reverend John Ramsbotham, to exorcise the premises; in his previous role as Bishop of Jarrow, Ramsbotham had successfully intervened in a poltergeist case in Sunderland, a story which had received a high media profile. Sadly, the outcome of his labours at Flockton is not recorded.

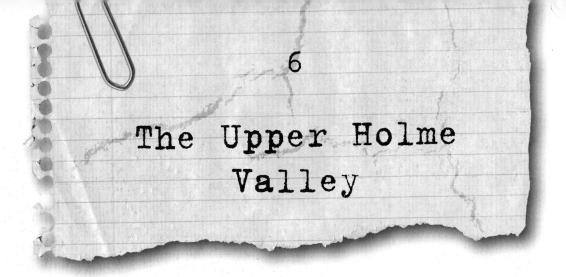

6

The Upper Holme Valley

A Meltham Miscellany

Situated at the northern edge of the Peak District National Park, for centuries Meltham remained a remote weaving community rarely troubled by developments beyond the next horizon. Then, in 1774, the Brooks of Newhouse Hall arrived from Sheepridge and proceeded to establish the first fulling mill in the village. The Industrial Revolution followed hard in its wake and by the latter half of the nineteenth century, Meltham Mills employed over 1,000 people, most of whom were housed in the burgeoning rows of terraces built by the philanthropic Brook family.

Although the majority of its industry has long since disappeared, Meltham remains a typical Pennine mill town. Victorian terraces sit uncomfortably alongside modern social housing, while its fringes straggle into bleak moorland beyond. Yet despite Meltham's relative mundanity, it has one of the highest concentrations of reported hauntings in the Huddersfield region. Indeed, the whole tract of upland countryside extending from the upper Holme Valley down towards Glossopdale in Derbyshire has long been recognised as a hotspot for paranormal activity. Some researchers have even dubbed this area the 'South Pennine Window'.

Face-Off

Dominated by the brooding mass of Wessenden Moor, Mill Moor Road can be an ominous place at the best of times and late on a stormy night in the depths of December, it is certainly not somewhere to linger. On just such a night in 1959, twenty-year-old Peter Crompton was walking down Mill Moor Road, returning home following a visit to some friends. Doubtless it was a dismal and lonely slog, walking alone in the early hours of the morning through a part of the town in which streetlights had yet to be installed.

Glancing nervously over his shoulder – as a person tends to do from time to time in such a situation – Crompton noticed a figure behind him, proceeding down the middle of the road. He stopped and waited for the follower to catch up, hoping to secure some company for the remainder of his journey home. However, as the tall, shadowy form drew closer, a

Mill Moor Road, Meltham – where a faceless horror chased a man in 1959.

singularly disconcerting feature emerged. The stranger had no face!

Upon seeing this, a profound sense of dread seized Crompton and he started to run as fast as his legs could carry him. Yet every time he summoned the courage to look back, the figure was still in pursuit. Such was his terror, he ran far beyond his home at Sunny Heys and it was not until he reached the electric lights of Station Road some distance away that he finally shook off whatever had been stalking him.

Mr Crompton's experience quickly became the talk of Meltham, with many residents concluding that the apparition must have emerged from a row of thirteen ancient cottages along Mill Moor Road which were being demolished in a project of slum clearance. Others dismissed the whole episode and insisted that it was simply an illusion created by scraps of paper or cloth carried on the air in the strong winds.

Both site manager Frank Butters and reporters from the *Huddersfield Daily Examiner* searched the cellars of the cottages in an attempt to quell the fears of the local populace. Nothing untoward was discovered, but the experience of Peter Crompton suggests that whatever once lurked in those cottages had already forsaken its condemned abode. And whilst today the buildings may have long since been demolished, perhaps once night has fallen that faceless horror prowls the streets of Meltham still.

Blithe Spirit

As the Netherton visitant demonstrated, a site does not necessarily have to be of any great antiquity to gain a reputation for being haunted. Often in such instances it seems that an individual who resides at the property is the focus of the spirit's attention, rather than the structure itself. This certainly seems to have been true in the case of a manifestation which troubled the Horn family at their home in Colders Green, a modern council house in Meltham, throughout the year of 1961.

The ghost was first witnessed by twenty-nine-year-old Betty Horn in the bedroom of her house on Good Friday, while her husband was out working a nightshift. She described the apparition as resembling a middle-aged woman of unusually lofty stature – well over 6 feet tall: 'It was big and horrid and touched me on the face with its hands. They were like a cold mist.' The spectre appeared to Mrs Horn three more times over the Easter period, before withdrawing for several months.

Despite her evident dismay, as a sceptic on the issue of the supernatural Arnold Horn had initially refused to believe his wife's account. On the night of 15 October, however, all that changed when he too was confronted by the ghost in his own bedroom. He said, 'I lashed out at it and it backed through the bedroom wall into the children's room. At the very point where it disappeared, my six-year-old daughter was sleeping. She screamed and ran frightened around the house.'

The Horns' five children were so traumatised by events, they had all moved into their parents' bedroom to sleep, although it was revealed that the ghost had been visiting their eight-year-old son for some considerable time. The boy explained that she would often sit on the end of his bed, massaging his legs whilst he told her about his day. His parents had often heard the child speaking to somebody at night but had always assumed that he was just talking in his sleep.

Over the course of the next week, two neighbours also witnessed the apparition

The house in Colders Green, Meltham.

at the bedroom window and, following a report on the haunting in the *Huddersfield Daily Examiner*, the house became something of a visitor attraction. Crowds of sightseers gathered outside day and night hoping to catch a glimpse of the ghost, whilst Mrs Horn found herself the object of superstitious gossip in the local shops.

By this point, the family were at the end of their tether and gladly accepted an offer of support from Hubert Saxon, a medium and president of the Huddersfield Spiritualist Church. Mr Saxon and several members of the church visited No. 9 Colders Green on 1 November to conduct a séance in the room where the ghost had been seen most frequently. During the ritual, Mr Saxon heard the name 'Annie' whispered by a disembodied voice and was directed towards a drawer in which he felt sure they would find something to identify the ghost.

From this information, the Horns concluded that the spirit belonged to Arnold's Aunt Annie, who had died nine years earlier and vaguely fitted the description of the apparition. They believed she must have returned to tend to their eight-year-old son, who at the age of two had contracted meningitis and lost the use of his legs for several years, only to mysteriously regain them in defiance of all medical opinion. Nonetheless, the family did not seem especially grateful for Annie's intervention and Mrs Horn baldly admitted, 'I hope that's the lot because ever since this thing started we've not had a moment's peace.'

Drums in the Deep

A far less benevolent haunting was experienced ten years later by twenty-five-year old George Borge at his rented one-up-one-down terrace on nearby Clarke Lane. Every Monday and Tuesday night, between two and three o'clock in the morning, he would be subjected to a barrage of seemingly supernatural disturbances which grew so terrifying that he was left unable to sleep, even with the aid of medication. On one occasion he was even forced to evacuate the house and pass the night in the waiting room of the town's railway station.

Typical poltergeist activity was experienced around the house generally, including mysterious footsteps, slamming doors, moving furniture and plates crashing onto the floor. However, the majority of the trouble seemed to be emanating from the cellar. In one instance, Borge witnessed the doorknob turn of its own accord, whilst his dog Jackie would often sit barking at the top of the cellar steps with her fur standing on end. More terrifyingly, he reported having heard the beating of drums and a blood-curdling woman's scream sound from the depths on several occasions.

No. 9 Clarke Lane, Meltham.

Borge told the *Huddersfield Daily Examiner* that he feared 'voodoo' was being practiced upon him and following this press report, several individuals contacted the newspaper, claiming they could discern a demonic face lurking in the shadows of the cellar in a photograph published alongside the article. Meanwhile, a woman known locally as Gypsy Nell came forward with a profoundly disconcerting tale. She claimed to have been told as a child that years before, the house had been the scene of a brutal double murder, only for the perpetrator to come to a sticky end himself in the cellar.

As Gypsy Nell told it, the house had once been occupied by a young couple who stole money from an elderly neighbour and concealed it in their cellar, beneath a flagstone covered by an old horsehair mattress. Somehow, another man came to learn of their secret and broke into the house one night in an attempt to recover the money. He was discovered by the woman living there and in attempt to silence her screams, he killed her and was forced to deal similarly with her husband when he came to his wife's aid.

However, the murderer did not know where the money was hidden and in his desperation to find it, he upturned furniture, threw crockery from the shelves and generally ransacked the house. Eventually his search took him to the cellar but he was unaware that the door could not be opened from within and whilst he was down there, it slammed shut, leaving him unable to escape. Nobody heard his banging and cries for help, until finally he died of starvation atop the horsehair mattress beneath which his goal remained secreted.

Certainly this story agreed with the details of the haunting, perhaps too well some might argue. Nonetheless, a few days later two 'psychical investigators' visited the house to see what they could ascertain. Along with George and his wife, Barbara, they first attempted to contact the spirits using a Ouija board. The planchette ominously spelled out 'Sam Dobson lived here. Stop the dog barking. There is money in the cellar'.

Several hours later they were joined by a number of journalists and as the habitual hour of the haunting approached, the vigil began in earnest. But despite some unusual temperature changes which even the pressmen were forced to acknowledge, nothing of significance occurred. The investigators suggested that simply by acknowledging the source of the haunting, it may have been exorcised, adding, 'There's definitely been some phenomena here. By the sensations we have picked up, there is no doubt about it – it is by no means a leg pull. Because of the sort of phenomena that it is, it must be somebody who died through tragic circumstances.'

Whatever the explanation, it is worth noting that all three hauntings discussed above occurred over a single decade within a very concentrated area of Meltham: Colders Green runs perpendicular to Mill Moor Road, whilst Clarke Lane is only a couple of streets away. Those of a sceptical persuasion might argue that it is evidence of little more than a bandwagon effect compounded by confirmation bias, whereby the idea of ghosts became so entrenched in the local psyche that perfectly explicable occurrences were interpreted in such terms.

Paranormal researchers, however, may wonder if there could have been some unified, objective cause behind the experiences. Some observers have posited that hauntings may be caused not by the spirits of the dead, but by anomalous natural forces not yet fully understood. Folk motifs such as 'ghosts' are then projected onto such phenomena by witnesses, in an attempt to make their abnormal experience comprehensible – to themselves and others. In view of the high density of paranormal reports from this region of the South Pennines generally, it is a hypothesis worth bearing in mind.

Thick Hollins, Meltham

During the Middle Ages it seems that Thick Hollins may have been a community in its own right, but by the sixteenth century it had become the seat of the local branch of the Armytage family (later the Green-Armytages), Lords of the Manor of Meltham. The hall still standing today was constructed around this time, albeit substantially renovated during the early 1800s.

The Green-Armytages dwelled at Thick Hollins for several centuries until 1841, when the scion of the dynasty took Holy Orders and leased the hall, first to the industrialist Brook family (formerly of Newhouse Hall at Sheepridge), then to the Carlile baronets. In 1908, it became home to the Meltham Golf Club, who established a course in the grounds whilst using the hall as their clubhouse. The estate was sold outright to the club ten years later and they are based there to this day.

Although the Green-Armytage family continued to own Thick Hollins between quitting their residency in 1841 and its eventual sale in 1918, they never once returned to the hall, despite repeated invitations from the Carlile family. Such strange, even discourteous behaviour was a source of considerable gossip in the neighbourhood during the late nineteenth century and was attributed to persecution by a supernatural presence which had not only driven the family from the hall but left them fearful to return.

Local tradition maintained it was the ghost of a mentally disturbed woman who

Thick Hollins Hall, Meltham.

had lived at Thick Hollins Hall during the 1820s, before her deteriorating condition had necessitated removal to an asylum. Her mania often manifested as an insatiable hunger for bizarre foods, leading to rumours that she even cooked and devoured babies. Whether this was a sincere superstition or a joking exaggeration, possibly employed by parents as a bogeyman with which to threaten their disobedient children, is not clear.

Local historian Philip Ahier did not find any evidence to support such a story, but whatever its cause, ostensibly supernatural phenomena was undoubtedly experienced at Thick Hollins. This was especially the case during the late nineteenth century and the tenancy of the Carlile family, who claimed to have regularly heard the sound of weeping from unoccupied rooms and disembodied footsteps echoing along deserted corridors.

Sir Walter Carlile (later Conservative MP for North Buckinghamshire) often stayed at the hall during his childhood and recalled once seeing the dogs recoil from some invisible threat, at which they continued to snarl for some time. On another occasion, a family member witnessed a woman dressed in black, with a white cap, enter a store-room in the house. Not recognising her as one of the servants, he followed her in, only to find the small room empty, despite there being no other means of egress.

The Ghost Flier of West Nab

The weathered gritstone outcrop at Wessenden Head, known as West Nab, ranks with Castle Hill as one of the most topographically significant features in the Huddersfield district; with Shooters Nab at the opposite end, it forms the western

Cock Crowing Stone, Meltham.

extremity of a prominent saddle on the horizon which can be seen from miles around. Up close, it is no less imposing. Cyclopean chunks of rock, weathered into strange and contorted forms, protrude from the summit like the shattered spine of some fallen leviathan.

Such is the wild and potent atmosphere of the place, in the nineteenth century an Upperthong clergyman and antiquarian by the name of Reverend H. G. Wilks, hypothesised that it had once been a 'Druidical Temple of the Sun', where the blood of sacrifices was caught in hollows in the rock. Whilst Wilks' theories have long since been discredited, it seems likely that the site was significant to prehistoric man nonetheless, for a number of Bronze Age and Romano-British earthworks can be found nearby.

Just below the summit of West Nab stands the mysterious Cock-Crowing Stone, a suggestively phallic boulder whose identification has been rendered effortless by the name painted in large white letters on its southern face. The exact etymology of the stone remains something of an enigma. No written folklore has survived, but from comparison with similar examples elsewhere in the country, it seems likely that it was formerly believed to spin round at cockcrow on some notable date in the calendar.

It was in the vicinity of this stone that in 1997 two birdwatchers had a strange experience, albeit one which is surprisingly common on the moors of the Dark Peak. Whilst crossing the boggy peat on the lookout for birds of prey, the pair were disturbed by the troubled sputtering of an engine nearby and, glancing skywards, they saw a shabby, out-of-control aircraft careening through the haze barely 100 feet above. They were close enough to see the pilot and vividly recall that beneath his goggles, he appeared to have no face. As if this was not disconcerting enough, moments later all evidence of the plane vanished completely.

As aviation enthusiasts, the witnesses were convinced the aircraft had been a Messerschmidt BF-109, notoriously used by the Luftwaffe during the Second World War. German planes undoubtedly flew over this area of the Pennines on bombing raids aimed at Manchester or Sheffield and whilst there is no record of a BF-109 running into difficulties, a Junkers Ju-88 is thought to have crashed around Saddleworth in 1941. A number of RAF planes also came down over the surrounding hills during the Second World War, including at Holme Moss, Redbrook Clough and Meltham Moor.

Phantom aircraft have proved a surprisingly common phenomenon in the northern Peak District over the last forty years. For instance, in 1982 and 1998 the image of a Lancaster bomber was seen over

West Nab, Meltham.

the Derwent reservoirs, an area famously used to train the RAF No. 617 Squadron for the 1943 'Dambuster' raids. There are only two such planes still operational and the RAF insist that neither have been flown over the area in recent decades.

Meanwhile, on the night of 24 March 1997, several credible witness, including farmers, gamekeepers and a police special constable, reported seeing an aircraft in difficulties over the Howden Moors (barely 10 miles from West Nab), followed by an explosion. Yet despite a fifteen-hour search covering 40 square miles and involving over 100 trained volunteers, tracker dogs and two helicopters, no crash site was ever found, nor were any planes reported missing by the aviation authorities.

Thongsbridge Mills, Thongsbridge

Although such things are typically associated with creaking old houses and desolate landscapes, the supernatural is also known to encroach upon more modern environments. Industrial folklore in Britain may be a lamentably under-researched topic but during the country's manufacturing heyday, there were few factories or mills without a resident spook. Often such manifestations were attributed to an operative who'd suffered some horrific accident in one of the machines or a past owner who'd hanged himself after getting into financial difficulties.

In the early 1970s, nightshift workers at R.L. Robinson Ltd, a dyeing firm which at the time occupied Thongsbridge Mills, were troubled by a series of disturbances which left some of their number afraid to enter certain rooms. Loud, unexplained crashes, 'as if someone had hit the floor above with a sledgehammer' frequently disturbed their concentration, whilst several employees encountered a strange vortex of mist which seemed to frequent a warehouse used for storing dried bales.

One anonymous witness described the apparition as a column of vapour several feet high, floating above the ground. He added, 'It's not a damp place and I don't think it could have been steam. It seemed to be spiralling within itself like cigarette smoke . . . I heard that another man saw it – then it appeared to have a light at the top. He said he pushed a bale right through it.'

Many of the mill hands ascribed the ghost to a former proprietor who'd committed suicide in the building. However, this story is apocryphal and, as mentioned previously, a suspiciously common motif in factory lore. Another possible hypothesis is that the ghost represented the restless spirit of Mr Jonathon Sandford, one of the most famous victims of the Great Holmfirth Flood.

At around one o'clock in the morning on 5 February 1852, the dam at Bilberry Reservoir burst following two weeks of torrential rain, sending 86 million gallons of water surging down the Holme Valley. Eighty-one people lost their lives, whilst houses, mills and bridges were all swept away. An inquiry later concluded that the flood had been caused by defects in the construction of the dam in 1840 and found the owners 'guilty of great and culpable negligence'. It remains one of the worst flooding disasters in British history.

Jonathon Sandford was a man of property who lived with his two young daughters at Dyson's Mill, located just below where the tributary from Bilberry Reservoir joins the River Holme. Despite advice regarding the condition of the dam, Sandford had chosen not to evacu-

R.L. Robinson Mill, Thongsbridge.

ate his family and inevitably none survived the inundation. It was fifteen days before Sandford's body was recovered, more than 2 miles downstream, deeply embedded in mud at the goit of Thongsbridge Mills. Such was the condition of the corpse, the man who found it had initially disregarded it, thinking it to be nothing more than a distended mass of bacon.

The Red Lion Inn, Jackson Bridge

The picturesque village of Jackson Bridge near Holmfirth is a familiar sight to many, having been extensively used as a shooting location for the long-running BBC sitcom *Last of the Summer Wine*. Indeed, the Red Lion pub is situated behind a row of cot-

tages featured in almost every episode as the homes of several major characters, and has itself been glimpsed in the series.

Converted into a beer house from two dwellings in the mid-nineteenth century, it was named the Red Lion in 1890 and, over the years, became one of the most popular hostelries in the area. However, during the 1970s and '80s it was famed for supernatural disturbances as much as the quality of its ale. Although no apparition was ever seen, poltergeist-type activity at the pub was rife and experienced by a number of witnesses.

When Mick Harper moved from Barnsley to take over the license at the Red Lion in 1983, he was soon confronted by inexplicable phenomena which left him at his wit's end. It began with loud crashes which woke him in the middle of the night and sent him running downstairs,

The Red Lion, Jackson Bridge.

convinced that an entire shelf of glasses had collapsed and shattered on the floor. On other occasions he discovered barrels rolling around in the cellar and ornamental plates seemingly flung from the walls.

When Mr Harper was forced to call a professional to service a brand new jukebox that repeatedly broke down, the engineer discovered three records entirely dislodged from the rack, something he insisted could only have occurred if the machine had been turned upside down. It malfunctioned again shortly afterwards and this time eighteen discs had mysteriously jumped from their slots.

As time wore on, the disturbances grew ever more kinetic and violent. Mr Harper emerged from the cellar one day to find several customers in a state of shock and a number of the pub's weighty brass ashtrays strewn across the floor. Malcolm Tinker of Scholes explained: 'Something just went bang. Ashtrays whizzed off the shelf and one of the lads threw himself to the ground.' His report was corroborated by David Mallinson of Hade Edge, who added, 'It was just like a twelve-bore shotgun going off.'

Several nights later, a similar episode occurred. Mr Harper and a number of regulars were enjoying a lock-in when suddenly the temperature in the bar dropped significantly and four ashtrays were hurled from the shelf. Moments afterwards, Mr Harper's sixteen-year-old son, Robert, ran down the stairs in terror. He told them, 'My room was filled by flashing yellow light, like flames. It was weird, there was no way I was staying in there.'

Following Mr Harper's plea to the local press for an explanation, a former landlord, who wished to remain anonymous, came forward to say he had also experienced phenomena during his tenure at the Red Lion. He recalled hearing inexplicable crashes and observing doors open and shut of their own accord. The ex-licensee even had a macabre theory as to what was causing the trouble; he attributed it to the ghost of Chippy Brook, one of his predecessors, who had hanged himself in the pub in 1947 following the collapse of his marriage.

Perhaps unsurprisingly, the Harper family remained at the Red Lion for less than two years and the owner, Tetley's Breweries, saw their departure as an appropriate juncture at which to sell the pub. When asked to comment on the haunting, their spokesman said, 'We've heard about the ghost. Our own theories are this was caused by electrical problems.' It was a hypothesis Mr Harper had long-since investigated and found wanting.

The Shoulder of Mutton, Holmfirth

Following the press exposure given to ghostly disturbances at the Red Lion in Jackson Bridge during the summer of 1984, reports also began to circulate concerning supernatural phenomena at this prominent three-storey pub in the heart of Holmfirth. Lodger Kevin Marah complained of sleepless nights due to door handles rattling and the sound of footsteps in empty rooms, experiences shared by a former lodger named Sandy King, and barmaid Joan Bottomley.

Marah believed this activity came from the unquiet spirit of a former landlady who'd died in his room fourteen years earlier and resented his presence. Her son, David Sykes, still resided at the pub and on one occasion after hours in the empty bar, he and Marah jokingly asked, 'Is there anybody there?' in the fashion of a séance. When three knocks rang out in return, the pair fled the pub in terror.

Taken in isolation, these experiences possibly seem like weak fare. However, two years later when the pub appeared in the newspapers again, the haunting had not only persisted but grown in intensity. This apparently followed the installation of new landlord, Glenn Hoyle, who had moved into the premises with his girlfriend Jo Greenwood and her two pre-school-age children, Emma and Eve.

At first the family encountered only the same low-level poltergeist activity as their predecessors, including mysterious footsteps, flickering lights and relocated furnishings in the bar, as if some force was attempting to rearrange the pub as it thought the place should be. Ms Greenwood also heard indistinct children's voices from the upper floor and complained that one of the rooms smelled permanently of festering vase water. Any flowers she attempted to place in the room would wither straight away.

When they tried to change the pub signs, the situation deteriorated. An old picture of the pub to which Mr Hoyle had attempted

The Shoulder of Mutton, Holmfirth.

to have a representation of the new signs professionally added was discovered in the middle of the bar – far from the wall on which it had hung – with its frame shattered. On another morning, a perfectly formed line of broken crockery was discovered on the kitchen floor.

The first visible manifestation of the phantom occurred when Mr Hoyle was woken at approximately half past four in the morning by a glow in his bedroom 'like a headlight in thick fog'. Looking over to the dressing table, he saw the figure of a woman from whom the light seemed to emanate. She was combing her hair with an old-fashioned brush, but cast no reflection in the dressing table mirror and after Mr Hoyle had watched her for several minutes, vanished into thin air.

Several nights later, the apparition was seen again by Jo's mother, Mavis Greenwood, whilst she was babysitting. Curiously, in a reversal of Mr Hoyle's experience, she saw the woman only as a reflection in a mirror. Mrs Greenwood added, 'I was just mesmerised by the sight. She moved very slightly towards me and I could see this very sad look on her face . . . I would quite like to see her again. I think I would ask why she looks so troubled.'

Perhaps most disturbing for the family was the effect the haunting seemed to have on Jo Greenwood's two-and-a-half-year-old daughter, Emma. Not only had the child reacted badly to the new environment – pulling down curtains and wallpaper and tearing up blankets – but she was also involved in several incidents which could not be so readily explained as a consequence of her awkward age.

On one occasion, she was found trapped in a wardrobe, the door of which only ever swung open rather than closed, whilst on another, she was discovered wandering the upstairs corridor with a pair of tin-snips attached to her dress. Emma had also developed a fascination for a particular window in an upper room of the pub and would repeatedly climb onto its sill, despite all admonishment, ultimately necessitating the installation of bars to prevent an accident. Whilst at the window, she seemed to be communing with some invisible presence.

Hoyle and Greenwood were ultimately forced to call on the services of a well-known local clairvoyant by the name of 'Shantoo', who informed the troubled couple that Emma was responding to the aura of a little boy who sought to become her playmate. Indeed, the medium believed the Shoulder of Mutton to be positively infested with earthbound spirits. In addition to the mournful woman combing her hair, he detected the presence of an entire band of uniformed men in the main bar, and an old lady 'dressed in pure black in a high-collared dress . . . with a lace cap and smoking a clay joss', sat in a corner notorious for its chill even when a fire was lit.

The identity of the spectres seemed easy enough to pinpoint. The medium agreed that much of the mischief in the pub had been caused by the ghost of the former landlady, unhappy with the alterations. Meanwhile, the uniformed men in the main bar were thought to be an impression of the Bolsterstone Male Voice Choir, eight of whom had been killed in a coach crash directly outside the pub on 19 October 1947 whilst travelling to a competition in the town. The medium claimed to have been previously unaware of this event.

As for the unhappy woman and the little boy, the most likely identification seems to be a twenty-three-year-old woman named Amelia Fearns and an unknown eleven-year-old male, who both drowned in the Great Holmfirth flood of 1852.

In the aftermath of the catastrophic deluge, many pubs in the district were employed as temporary mortuaries and several corpses were brought to the Shoulder of Mutton, including the two unfortunate individuals aforementioned.

Black Syke Reservoir, Holmfirth

Nestling in the hollow of Hart Holes Clough just below the Ford Inn on Greenfield Road, Black Syke Reservoir was constructed as a dam on Black Sike Dyke in order to provide water and power for a nearby mill, now long since demolished. These waters have always had a sinister reputation. Permanently crouched in the shadow of the surrounding hillsides and overhung by dense vegetation, it is a bleak and forbidding place, an atmosphere only compounded by knowledge of the tragedies which have occurred in its environs.

In 1820, Black Syke was responsible for one of Holmfirth's several great floods when a period of heavy and prolonged rain caused the dam to burst, sending a torrent of water gushing towards the town,

Black Syke Dam, Holmfirth.

causing injuries and substantial destruction of property. The reservoir was also a notorious spot for suicides and only days before the experience recounted below, the body of thirty-nine-year-old William Carter, a Holme Bridge farmer known to have been suffering from depression, was dragged from its murky depths.

Despite the grim character of the place, during the 1920s and '30s it was a popular spot for night swimming amongst those in their late teens and early twenties. One night in October 1930, a group calling themselves the Moonlight Bathers had braved the brisk conditions to enjoy their pastime at the reservoir, and as was customary following a swim, the sexes had divided to opposite banks of the water to dress amongst the trees.

It was at this point that two men, separated from the rest of the group, beheld an extraordinary sight. They described witnessing 'the outline of a deathly looking white horse pulling a shandy, moving slowly across the water on the other side of the dam'. The astonished pair continued to watch it for several moments before it seemed to disappear amongst the shadow of the trees on the north bank of the reservoir.

A local tradition held that many years earlier, a horse drawing a cart had taken fright and careered into the reservoir to drown, and following the bathers' sighting, crowds of people began to congregate at Black Syke, hoping to observe the ghost for themselves. Whilst many others claimed to have seen the phantom, the *Huddersfield Daily Examiner* remained sceptical and, following a visit to the dam, their reporter concluded it was nothing more than a tattered white sheet caught on the branches of a tree. Few, however, were convinced.

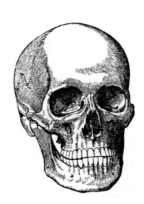

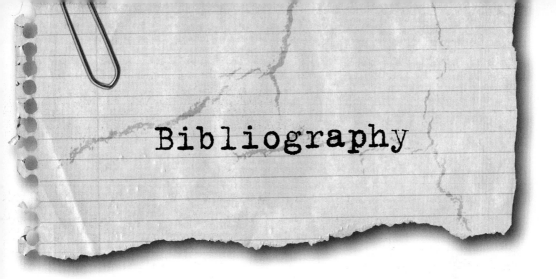

Bibliography

Books

Ahier, Philip, *Newhouse Hall and Its Associations in the Manor of Huddersfield* (Advertiser Press, 1934)

Ahier, Philip, *Legends and Traditions of Huddersfield and Its District* (Advertiser Press, 1943–4)

Ahier, Philip, *The Story of Castle Hill* (Advertiser Press, 1946)

Bennett, Paul, *The Old Stones of Elmet* (Capall Bann, 2001)

Billingsley, John, *A Stoney Gaze: Investigating Celtic and Other Stone Heads* (Capall Bann, 1998)

Billingsley, John, *West Yorkshire Folk Tales* (The History Press, 2010)

Clarke, David, *Supernatural Peak District* (Robert Hale, 2000)

Cliffe, Steve, *Shadows: A Northern Investigation of the Unknown* (Sigma Publications, 1993)

Cunniff, Tom, *The Supernatural in Yorkshire* (Dalesman Books, 1985)

Davies, Owen, *The Haunted: A Social History of Ghosts* (Palgrave MacMillan, 2007)

Easther, Alfred, *A Glossary of the Dialect of Almondbury and Huddersfield* (English Dialect Society, 1883)

Hobkirk, Charles, *Huddersfield: Its History and Natural History* (Minerva Press, 1868)

Linahan, Liz, *Pit Ghosts, Padfeet and Poltergeists* (The King's England Press, 1994)

Mitchell, W.R., *Haunted Yorkshire* (Dalesman Books, 1990)

Moorehouse, Henry James, *The History and Topography of the Parish of Kirkburton* (H. Roebuck, 1861)

Owens, Andy, *Yorkshire Stories of the Supernatural* (Countryside Books, 1999)

Owens, Andy, *Paranormal West Yorkshire* (The History Press, 2008)

Pobjoy, Reverend H.N., *A History of Emley* (Ridings Publishing, 1970)

Roberts, Andy, *Ghosts and Legends of Yorkshire* (Jarrold Publishing, 1992)

Schofield, Isobel, *Aspects of Huddersfield* (Wharncliffe Books, 1999)

Simpson, Jacqueline & Roud, Steve, *A Dictionary of English Folklore* (Oxford University Press, 2000)

Sykes, John, *Slawit in the Sixties* (Schofield & Sims, 1923)

Various, *Memories of Thurstonland and Stocksmoor* (St Thomas Church Committee, 2000)

Wade, Stephen, *Hauntings in Yorkshire* (Halsgrove, 2008)

Newspapers

Colne Valley Chronicle
The Dalesman
Halifax Courier and Guardian
Holme Valley Express
Huddersfield Chronicle
Huddersfield Daily Examiner
Fortean Times
Northern Earth
Yorkshire Post

A complete list of bibliographical references for each individual entry can be found at http://hauntedhuddersfield.wordpress.com

Other titles published by The History Press

Haunted Yorkshire Dales
SUMMER STREVENS

The beautiful, rolling hills of the Yorkshire Dales have long been a haven for holiday makers. However, the area also harbours some disturbing secrets. Discover the darker side of the Dales with this terrifying collection of true-life tales from across the region. Containing many accounts which have never before been published, and featuring chapters on ecclesiastic ectoplasms, ghostly creatures, ladies in black and star-crossed spooks, this book is guaranteed to make your blood run cold.

978 0 7524 5887 8

Yorkshire Villains: Rogues, Rascals and Reprobates
MARGARET DRINKALL

Discover the darker side of Yorkshire with this remarkable collection of true-life crimes from across the county

Featuring tales of highwaymen, cut throats, poachers, poisoners, thieves and murderers, all factions of the criminal underworld are included in this macabre selection of tales. Drawing on a wide variety of historical sources and containing many cases which have never before been published, *Yorkshire Villains* will fascinate everyone interested in true crime and the history of Yorkshire.

978 0 7524 6002 4

Haunted Rotherham
RICHARD BRAMALL & JOE COLLINS

This fascinating book contains a terrifying collection of true-life tales from in and around Rotherham. Featuring stories such as the Lunatic of Ulley Reservoir and the Old Hag of Hellaby Hall, this pulse-raising compilation of unexplained phenomena, apparitions, poltergeists, curses, spirits and boggards is guaranteed to make your blood run cold. Drawing on historical and contemporary sources, *Haunted Rotherham* will delight everyone interested in the paranormal.

978 0 7524 6117 5

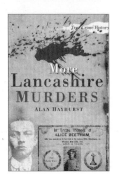

More Lancashire Murders
ALAN HAYHURST

In this follow-up to *Lancashire Murders*, Alan Hayhurst brings together more murderous tales that shocked not only the county but made headline news throughout the nation. They include the case of Oldham nurse Elizabeth Berry, who poisoned her own daughter in 1887; Margaret Walber, who beat her husband to death in Liverpool in 1893; and John Smith, the young Home-Guardsman who shot his ex-girlfriend in broad daylight at Whitworth in 1941. Alan Hayhurst's well-illustrated and enthralling text will appeal to everyone interested in the shady side of Lancashire's history.

978 0 7524 5645 4

Visit our website and discover thousands of other History Press books.

www.thehistorypress.co.uk

The History Press